PRAISE FC
THE LITTLE BOOK OF BIG COACHING MODELS

'All of our managers were given copies of *The Little Book of Big Management Theories*. It has become our workplace bible. We have over 100 full-time and volunteer coaches, mentors and support workers working for YSS who we will recommend this book to.'
Lorraine Preece – Chief Executive, YSS Training

'Like Bob's first book, this should be essential reading for all busy managers who want to get the best out of their workforce.'
Alan Shaw – Managing Director, Regent Engineering

'I have a bookshelf of management and coaching books. Bob's first book has pride of place. I look forward to the next one.'
Jo Morgan – Managing Director, Charlie's Training Academy

'Just a joy to read: Funny in parts, sad in others but always thought-provoking.'
Manny Sandhu – Director, Ubique

'We will use this book for all of our coaching sessions.'
John Curtis – CEO, Peer Support Programme

'It has been a pleasure to work with Bob. His work in coaching the village management team in the Gambia has been wonderful. I have recommended his book to colleagues at Banjul University as essential reading.'
Ibrahim Jallow – Chair, The Wonder Years Centre of Excellence (Gambia)

'Bob has been inspirational in helping us to provide a quality coaching and peer support service to ex-servicemen. I can't wait for his book to come out.'
Len Hardy – Director, The Veterans Contact Point

'I would strongly recommend that anybody completing either a CMI or ILM Level 5 Diploma in Leadership and Management should have this book.'
Chris Hooper – Training and Development Director, Eurosource Solutions

THE LITTLE
BOOK OF BIG
COACHING
MODELS

Bob Bates

THE LITTLE
BOOK OF BIG
COACHING
MODELS

76 WAYS TO HELP MANAGERS
GET THE BEST OUT OF PEOPLE

PEARSON

Harlow, England • London • New York • Boston • San Francisco • Toronto • Sydney
Auckland • Singapore • Hong Kong • Tokyo • Seoul • Taipei • New Delhi
Cape Town • São Paulo • Mexico City • Madrid • Amsterdam • Munich • Paris • Milan

Pearson Education Limited
Edinburgh Gate
Harlow CM20 2JE
United Kingdom
Tel: +44 (0)1279 623623
Web: www.pearson.com/uk

First published 2015 (print and electronic)

© Bob Bates 2015 (print and electronic)

The right of Bob Bates to be identified as author of this work has been asserted by him in accordance with the Copyright, Designs and Patents Act 1988.

Pearson Education is not responsible for the content of third-party internet sites.

ISBN: 978-1-292-08149-6 (print)
       978-1-292-08151-9 (PDF)
       978-1-292-08152-6 (ePub)
       978-1-292-08150-2 (eText)

British Library Cataloguing-in-Publication Data
A catalogue record for the print edition is available from the British Library

Library of Congress Cataloging-in-Publication Data
Bates, Bob, 1951-
  The little book of big coaching models : 76 ways to help managers get the best out of people
  / Bob Bates. -- 1st Edition.
     pages cm
  Includes index.
  ISBN 978-1-292-08149-6
  1. Employees--Coaching of. 2. Industrial management. I. Title.
  HF5549.5.C53B38 2015
  658.3'124--dc23
                          2014045824

10 9 8 7 6 5 4 3 2 1
19 18 17 16 15

Cover design by redeyoffdesign.com

Print edition typeset in Helvetica Neue LT Pro 9.5 by 3
Print edition printed in Great Britain by Henry Ling Ltd, at the Dorset Press, Dorchester, Dorset

NOTE THAT ANY PAGE CROSS REFERENCES REFER TO THE PRINT EDITION

For Irene and Charles

CONTENTS

PART 2 TAKING IT FURTHER

ABOUT THE AUTHOR

Bob Bates was a senior executive in the Civil Service for 20 years. During this time, he also worked as an employment coach and mentor to people with disabilities. He then set up his own management and training consultancy (The Arundel Group), which celebrates its twentieth anniversary this year. His work as a management consultant covered a number of local and central government projects as well as working with major UK private sector companies.

Bob had a break from consultancy in the late 1990s to take up a lecturing career, during which time he gained two Masters Degrees in management and a PhD in education and management. He has taught over 1,000 managers and teachers on graduate and post-graduate programmes at two universities.

This is Bob's second book. His first, *The Little Book of Big Management Theories* (Pearson, 2013), written with Jim McGrath was on WH Smiths' non-fiction best sellers list for nearly a year and is being translated into 10 languages.

Bob shares his time these days between writing, working as a chief executive for a charity that promotes health and education in the Gambia and teaching adult education teachers and probation service coaches and mentors. In the Gambia, he is currently coaching and mentoring a local management group to help them to take the village towards self-sufficiency.

Bob can be contacted by email on **saddlers9899@aol.com**.

ACKNOWLEDGEMENTS

A coach would be severely limited with no experience from the receiving end of the principles and tools of coaching. I'd therefore like to thank the many people who knowingly or unknowingly have helped me with this book. These include the many coaches, good and bad, who have been an influence on my life.

I have great memories of Les Still, my sports coach at school, who was probably the only reason why I stayed on to do A Levels. I also valued the support of Dr Paul Davies at Aston University who coached me through my Masters Degree and Professor David Hellawell who did likewise through my PhD.

I also owe a big vote of thanks to the many people who I've coached over the years who in turn taught me so much. A number of them are used as case studies in this book.

Thanks to Chris Bates for helping out with the diagrams.

Finally, a BIG word of thanks to Eloise Cook, Lucy Carter and the team at Pearson for turning my dream of being a writer into a reality.

To all of these people I offer my heartfelt thanks.

PUBLISHER'S ACKNOWLEDGEMENTS

We are grateful to the following for permission to reproduce copyright material:

Theory 3 figure from *Experiential Learning: Experience as the Source of Learning and Development*, Prentice Hall (Kolb, D.A. 1984), © 1984. Reprinted and electronically reproduced by permission of Pearson Education, Inc., Upper Saddle River, New Jersey; Theory 9 figure adapted from *Games People Play: The Psychology of Human Relationships*, Penguin (Berne, E. 1964); Theory 17 figure from 'A theory of human motivation', *Psychological Review* 50(4), pp. 370–96 (Maslow, A.H. 1943), reprinted with permission from the American Psychological Association; Theory 30 figure from *Changing Belief Systems with Neuro-Linguistic Programming [NLP]*, Meta Publications (Dilts, R. 1990), Meta Publications, P.O. Box 1910, Capitola, CA 95010, USA. E-mail: metapub@prodigy.net, website: **www.meta-publications.com**; Theory 47 figure from *The Tao of Coaching*, Profile Books (Landsberg, M. 2003), Profile Books Ltd; Theory 60 figure from *Theory in Practice: Increasing Professional Effectiveness*,

Jossey-Bass (Argyris, C. and Schön, D. 1974), republished with permission of John Wiley & Sons, Inc., permission conveyed through Copyright Clearance Center, Inc.; Theory 62 figure from *Organizational Culture and Leadership*, Jossey-Bass (Schein, E.H. 1992), republished with permission of John Wiley & Sons, Inc., permission conveyed through Copyright Clearance Center, Inc.; Theory 66 figure from 'Structure is not an organization', *Business Horizons* 23(3), pp. 14–26 (Waterman, R.H., Peters, T.J. and Phillips, J.R. 1980), with permission from Elsevier; Theory 67 figure from 'Marketing strategies and organisation structures for service firms', in *Marketing of Services*, pp. 47–51 (Booms, B.H. and Bitner, M.J. 1981 (Donnelly, J. and George, W.R., eds)), American Marketing Association, republished with permission of American Marketing Association, permission conveyed through Copyright Clearance Center, Inc.; Theory 73 figure from John Fisher's process of transition diagram, **http://www.businessballs.com/freepdfmaterials/processoftransitionJF2012.pdf**, with permission from Businessballs and John M. Fisher.

In some instances we have been unable to trace the owners of copyright material, and we would appreciate any information that would enable us to do so.

HOW TO USE THIS BOOK

This book will:

- help you to understand what makes people tick;
- develop your skills as a coach;
- enable you to get the best out of your people;
- encourage you and your people to have a commitment to personal growth and change.

It is for managers who want to get the best out of their people through coaching and has a variety of tools that any manager can easily use, no matter what the business purpose.

People are the most important aspect of any organisation and yet many managers look on external training as the best way of developing their employees. This can often be a costly and time-consuming exercise in which someone's initial enthusiasm for the training dwindles and they fail to apply newly found knowledge or skills. Having someone available on hand with the right aptitude, skills and knowledge to support and encourage them is the best way to get the best out of people.

This book is easy to use but effective. It is written for busy managers who are more interested in solutions to problems and the application of a theory rather than a critical analysis of the theory. It describes each theory and model in less than 350 words and its application in less than 500 words.

This is the unique selling point for this book. You simply decide what issue you need to resolve, look up the appropriate sections in the book that deal with this issue and choose which one(s) will help you.

The book is divided into three parts:

- **Part 1** covers the knowledge and techniques you must have to get started as a coach.
- **Part 2** looks at more advanced theories and contemporary models of coaching.
- **Part 3** looks at coaching the organisation.

Each part is broken down into a number of sections covering typical everyday managerial tasks, which in turn are made up of a number of theories and models from well-known thinkers in that field.

INTRODUCTION

WHAT YOU WILL GET FROM THIS BOOK

This book is written with not just managers and coaches in mind but mentors, teachers, trainers and counsellors of any individuals or groups who want to understand more about how people think and why they do the things they do and more importantly how to use this understanding to get the best out of people.

This book doesn't attempt to trivialise great theory or models through its brevity on each subject, but it does recognise that managers, coaches and the people they are working with are very busy people and may not have the time to devote to reading Carl Rogers' *On Becoming a Person* (Constable, 2004) or John Whitmore's *Coaching for Performance* (Nicholas Brealey, 1998). My aim is to explain the various theories or models as succinctly as possible and provide what's very often missing in academic works, how you apply these tools in practice.

The book is divided into three parts:

- **Part 1** covers the knowledge and techniques managers must have to get started as a coach and includes: understanding how people think and learn; what motivates them to want to learn; telling them what to do; showing them what they need to do; suggesting ways they can do it; and stimulating them to do it. Although they are presented in a very simplified format, the theories underpinning these models are quite profound and based on the work of famous thinkers in the field.

- **Part 2** looks at more advanced theories and contemporary models of coaching. This part is for managers who have worked through the basic models and want to develop their skills as a coach further. It is also useful for existing coaches, mentors or teachers who want to improve their practice. This is a toolbox for managers who want a tried and tested systematic process that they can use for coaching.

- **Part 3** looks at coaching the organisation. This part is for managers who want to improve the performance of their organisation through coaching and covers the key aspects of organisational behaviour including: leadership, culture, planning, quality, change and team working.

Each part is broken down into a number of sections covering typical everyday managerial tasks, which in turn are made up of a number of theories and models from well-known thinkers in that field. Each model or theory will be explained and made practical for managers. I've used a number of different approaches in the *how to use it* entries:

- **Tasks and tips** – a simple no nonsense step-by-step approach that you can follow in order to apply the theory or model. These will be indicated with a small black square.
- **Reflection points and challenges** – encouraging you to reflect on real-life case studies, problems or extracts from the world of sport or the cinema in order to develop your understanding of how to apply the theory or model. These are in grey boxes.
- **Analogies and metaphors** – taking you out of the real world for just a moment (including the odd trip to the cinema) and getting you to relate the theory to something which appears to have no apparent bearing on the theory or model but from which understanding and meaning can be drawn.
- **Questions to ask yourself** – each entry will have between one and four questions that you need to ask yourself before, during or after applying the theory or model.

HOW IS COACHING DIFFERENT FROM OTHER MEASURES?

It's important to locate coaching in respect of the various human resource development approaches that can take place in an organisation. A good starting point is to use the metaphor of *learning to drive* (my use of metaphors is something that you will have to get used to if you are going to get the best out of this book).

- A *consultant* will advise you on the most appropriate car to drive.
- A *counsellor* will try to address any anxieties that you have about driving.
- A *mentor* will share their own driving experiences with you.
- A **coach** will encourage you to get in and drive the car correctly.

The measures can be represented in terms of Challenging, Supporting, Directive and Non-directive in the following diagram:

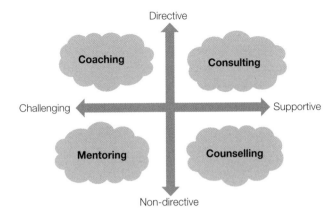

The one thing that unites each of the above approaches is that they seek some form of behaviour modification in either the organisation or the individual. The thing that differentiates coaching from other measures is the level of challenge and direction that takes place: challenge in respect of getting people to deliver the desired outcomes; direction in terms of telling them what to do or getting them to think and do it for themselves.

In the book, I make use of the term *desired state* to describe the outcome of coaching. If you are teaching someone to drive, the *desired state* is that they can get from A to B effectively and efficiently. I prefer to use this term because the use of *state* infers movement from one position to another and *desire* as the motivation to get there. If the purpose of the coach is to support the person to move towards their desired state, then it's understandable that you might think that coaching, mentoring or teaching are the same thing. It's important therefore that I discuss the differences in each of the approaches in terms of relationships, time, structure and outcome.

Teachers are usually trained professionals who work with people on developing their understanding of an issue. Coaches are also usually trained professionals but focus more on helping the person to develop specific skills. Mentors are usually experienced individuals who share knowledge and experiences with a less experienced person.

Mentoring requires time to develop a relationship of mutual trust in which both partners can learn about one another and feel safe in sharing the real issues that the person is facing. Teaching and coaching can be as short as a single session or part of a session that may be necessary for the person to develop understanding or a particular skill.

Teachers set the topic, the pace and the learning methods to help develop understanding. Coaches will respond to the individual's needs but may have a set structure to their approach. Mentors will tailor their approaches to meet the individual's needs.

Coaching and teaching are task oriented with the focus on concrete issues and easy-to-measure performance output. Mentoring is relationship oriented with the focus on mutual development.

While I'm on definitions, I dislike using the term 'coachee', so I simply use the term 'person being coached'. In Part 3 I use 'client' because this is appropriate when addressing a person/organisation commissioning the coaching.

Whichever approach you adopt, you need to have the basic belief that the person/people that you are working with:

- has the ability to change;
- will make the best choice available to them.

Supporting them to reach their desired state is more of a journey in which the process of learning is as important as the knowledge and skills gained.

Coaching is very much a pragmatic trade, drawing on borrowed theory which, to many, plays a much smaller role in coaching practice. Some would argue that practice leads theory and that coaching is *a-theoretical*. This book will bridge the gap between theory and practice.

I have been a coach and trainer with some very big national companies, some sole-trading organisations, voluntary bodies and individuals for over 40 years. The one thing that I've found out is that a lot of managers, coaches and learners struggle with how to apply theory to practice. This is what this book is all about.

PART 1

MAKING A START

INTRODUCTION

A s a manager you have a tough job. You are probably under intense pressure to achieve results, often with too few resources in terms of time and money. I suspect that this has always been the case but never more so than in the present day with a pace of change that's bewildering and a level of competition that's fierce. You have one key asset that makes your task less daunting and that's your people. Nothing will allow you to achieve more than having a skilled and motivated team working alongside you.

The ability to raise the performance of your team is an important element of being a good manager. Through effective coaching you can develop the people around you to take on more responsibility thus freeing yourself up to deal with the other aspects of management such as strategic planning and budgeting. It's important however to make the point at the very beginning of this part of the book that good coaching is a skill that requires a depth of understanding and plenty of practice if you want it to pay dividends for you, your organisation and the people you are coaching. Sadly, the converse is true and managers who go through the motions of coaching fail to achieve the intended results.

Okay, so by picking up this book you realise that you have a responsibility for developing people (individuals or groups) and want to do something about it. This may be something new for you or you may have been doing it for years. A word of warning! There are many different approaches to coaching: some that are subject-specific; some that are more general; some that rely on directing; and some more geared to supporting. In this respect, there is a spectrum of coaching styles that can be categorised as falling in either the *push* or *pull* approach. These will be covered in Part 1 and include:

- directing
- showing
- facilitating
- stimulating.

Before I look at the different coaching styles there are, however, some fundamental skills that you need to master in order to be a good coach, regardless of the approach you adopt. These are the abilities to listen attentively, communicate effectively, determine the appropriate performance goals and gauge the right buttons to push. I'll cover how you can develop these skills in the first four sections in this part of the book.

Of course, not all coaching sessions will run smoothly and you may be faced with difficult individuals to deal with. There may be situations when you face resistance to even your best coaching efforts. I've finished this part of the book with a look at three theories where dealing with challenging behaviour is the order of the day, culminating with a look at extreme or psychopathic behaviour and how to handle it.

All of the entries used in this part are taken from some of the great thinkers who have contributed to our understanding of how people learn and the most effective ways of supporting this learning.

SECTION 1

UNDERSTAND HOW PEOPLE THINK AND LEARN

INTRODUCTION

I t's important as a coach that you have a good understanding of how people think and learn. A learning style can be described as the idiosyncratic way in which an individual acquires, processes, comprehends and retains information. It's now widely accepted that each individual has a different learning style preference and that this preference can either be a dominant feature apparent in all learning situations, one that may vary according to circumstances or one that blends in with other learning styles. What is certain is that there is no single blueprint for learning styles that fits every individual in every situation.

I've chosen three different learning style theories that look at learning as being influenced by either the learner's senses, past experiences or personality. Each of the learning style theories has a questionnaire that you can use to determine your own preferred style of learning as well as that of the person you are coaching. Some of these are available free online, others you will have to pay for. The good news is that most of the ones you have to pay for contain a licence that allows you to copy and use with other people. I would suggest that, by trying them out first, you will get an idea of any problems or pitfalls that may occur when you use them with others. The important thing is not to be fazed if you turn out to be an *extroverted kinaesthetic pragmatist* (although I'd hate to bump into you in a dark alley!).

Before looking at the different learning styles, it's important to understand how people learn best and whether there are any distinctions according to the person's age. *Pedagogy* and *andragogy* are theories that hold a set of assumptions about how children and adults learn. The word *pedagogy* comes from the ancient Greek *Paidagogos*, who was the slave who supervised the education of slave children in whatever given trade they were forced into. It was the *Paidagogos'* job to act as a 'Drill Sergeant', and ensure that the slaves performed their daily routines as expected by their master. *Andragogy*, as a study of adult learning, originated in Europe in the 1950s and was then pioneered as a theory and model of adult learning from the 1970s by Malcolm Knowles, who defined *andragogy* as 'the art and science of helping adults learn'. An appreciation of Knowles' ideas will be the starting point for this section. This is followed by three classic theories that relate learning to the senses, experience and personality.

THEORY 1 # MALCOLM KNOWLES: HOW ADULTS LEARN

Use this when you want to understand how the basic principles of how adults learn will impact on your coaching strategy.

Knowles argued that most adult learners are autonomous and want to be in control of their learning. He maintained that, as an individual matures, the motivation to learn is driven more by inner desire (intrinsic motivators) rather than external stimuli (extrinsic motivators). He identified four basic assumptions that underpin adult learning:

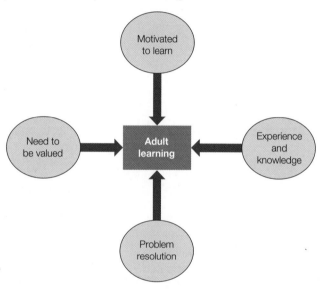

He suggested the following principles that characterise the differences between adult learning and traditional notions of *pedagogy*.

THESE ARE THAT ADULT LEARNERS:
are internally motivated, have their own particular views of themselves and their needs and are goal-oriented in terms of meeting those needs;
bring a vast array of life experiences and knowledge which can be a valuable resource for learning;
are practical and more concerned with learning in order to complete tasks or solve problems than just learning subjects;
like to have their contributions valued and respected.

Knowles emphasised the value of the process of learning that uses approaches that are problem-based and collaborative rather than didactic. He also argued for the need for more equality between the teacher/coach and learner in terms of choosing the content and style of delivery. Knowles acknowledged that, while not all learners are at the adult learner stage, it is important that the coach encourages them to take on more of the characteristics of an adult learner.

HOW TO USE IT

Here's how to interpret Knowles's ideas on adult learning:

- Start by actively involving them in setting the goals for the coaching experience. Be aware that not all of them will jump at the opportunity to be involved in this way. In order to facilitate their movement towards more self-direction you need to establish rapport with them and show genuine interest in their thoughts and opinions.

- Accept that most people thrive on the opportunity to share their knowledge and experiences. Find out about their interests and past experiences and support them to draw on these when working individually or in a group.

- Recognise that they are motivated to learn when they can see the need to acquire knowledge or skills to address a real-life problem or situation. Use real-life case studies as a basis from which to help them do this.

- Demonstrate your respect for them by taking an interest in them, acknowledging their contributions and encouraging them to express their ideas at every opportunity, even if you disagree with them.

QUESTIONS TO ASK YOURSELF

- Am I making sure that the people I am coaching can relate the coaching to their own goals, knowledge and experience?

- How good am I at understanding what really interests the person I am coaching?

THEORY 2 NEIL FLEMING: VAK

Use this when you want to understand the role that senses play in the coaching process.

Fleming's *visual*, *auditory*, *kinaesthetic* (VAK) model of learning styles has become one of the most widely used assessments of learning styles. Fleming argues that most people possess a dominant or preferred learning style that is based on either seeing, listening or doing.

THE DESCRIPTIONS FOR THESE CAN BE SUMMARISED AS:

Visual learners: Tend to learn through seeing, thinking in pictures and creating mental images to retain information.

Auditory learners: Tend to learn through listening, thinking in words rather than pictures and learning best through lectures and group discussions.

Kinaesthetic learners: Tend to learn through doing, expressing themselves through movement and learning best through interacting with others and the space around them.

Fleming argued that, although demonstrating a preference for one style, some people have a mixed and balanced blend of all three styles.

HOW TO USE IT

This is probably the most used of all learning style assessments and there are numerous online tests for this. The most common one is made up of a number of statements (usually around a dozen) with three possible responses which indicate a preference for one of the three styles. Here are a few tips to help you out with planning coaching that caters for people with each preference:

- Someone with a *visual* learning style may have a preference for seen or observed things so, in your coaching, make sure that you include pictures, diagrams, demonstrations, displays, hand-outs or films. Also, be aware that visual learners will use phrases such as 'show me', 'let's have a look at that' and will be best able to perform a new task after reading the instructions or observing someone else doing it first.

- Someone with an *auditory* learning style may have a preference for listening to the spoken word or sounds and noises. These people will use phrases such as 'tell me', 'let's discuss it' and will be best able to perform a new task after listening to instructions from the coach.

- Someone with a *kinaesthetic* learning style has a preference for physical experiences including touching, feeling, holding, doing. These people will use phrases such as 'let me try it', 'can I have a go at that' and will be best able to perform a new task by going ahead and trying it out, learning as they go. These are the people who like practical hands-on experiences so, as their coach, make sure that you give them every opportunity to do this.

Don't fall into the trap of thinking that, with someone who has a particular preference, your coaching approach should only cater for their preferred style. There is a good deal of virtue in helping these people to develop other learning styles as not all information they are ever presented with will be in their preferred style.

QUESTIONS TO ASK YOURSELF

- Am I taking account of someone's preferred learning style in my coaching material?
- Do I make sure that I expose them to other learning styles as well as their preferred one?

DAVID KOLB: EXPERIENTIAL LEARNING CYCLE

Use this when you want a process to ensure that learning takes place.

Kolb maintained that learning through experience will only happen if we process that experience and make sense of it. He argued that an experience on its own was insufficient to facilitate learning and needed to be followed by reflection on what happened, thoughts about what might happen if you did it differently and active experimentation on doing something differently and testing the results. He described the process as a cyclical model that is usually represented as:

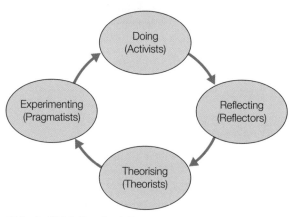

Source: Kolb, D. (1984) *Experiential Learning: Experience as the Source of Learning and Development*. Englewood Cliffs, NJ: Prentice-Hall.

Kolb described the characteristics of people who have a preference for a particular learning style.

THESE CHARACTERISTICS ARE:

Activists: Open-minded and enthusiastic, they are not afraid to try out something new.

Reflectors: Meticulous, they like to consider why things happen in the way that they do.

Theorists: Thinkers who like to come up with fresh insights into problems.

Pragmatists: Experimenters who are keen to make use of new ideas.

Kolb explains that there is no set fixed point of entry onto the cycle (for example if the individual's preferred learning style is as a theorist, they will start at that point) but that learning will only take place if an individual continues through each part of the cycle.

HOW TO USE IT

This is a simple, durable and effective model for thinking about learning and one that can provide a sturdy framework for planning coaching. There are numerous tests for determining an individual's preferred learning style. The most common one, the Learning Styles Questionnaire (LSQ), was devised by Alan Mumford and Peter Honey and consists of 80 statements which you either accept as being like you or reject as not being like you. The statements that you have given a positive response to are entered onto a grid that corresponds with the four learning styles. People completing the LSQ will generally have a preference for one or possibly two styles.

A working understanding of learning styles is helpful in planning a coaching session so here are a few tips to help you out with this:

Learning style	How to coach them
Activists	Expose them to new experiences: they like being thrown in at the deep end.
Reflectors	Allow them to stand back and listen and observe before acting: they like to ponder on a task.
Theorists	Work on ideas and abstract concepts with them: they excel at learning wide-ranging information and organising it in a clear logical format.
Pragmatists	Work on technical tasks with them and allow them to experiment with new ideas: they learn best by working with practical applications.

Use this theory in tandem with Honey and Mumford's LSQ. I strongly advise you at the start to do the LSQ to find out what your preference as a learner is. I have found that many coaches adopt a coaching style that mirrors their learning style. There's no problem with this providing the exercises chosen suit the learning style of the individual.

QUESTIONS TO ASK YOURSELF

- Do I let my own learning style preference dictate how I coach others?
- Am I making sure that the person I am coaching goes through all stages in the experiential learning cycle?

THEORY 4 KATHERINE MYERS AND ISABEL BRIGGS: THE MYERS-BRIGGS TYPE INDICATOR

Use this when you want to understand the role that personality plays in the coaching process.

The Myers-Briggs Type Indicator (MBTI) is built on four different scales, first suggested by Carl Jung, as a way to describe personality types. Myers and Briggs proposed that each individual displayed personality traits that were at either end of a series of scales:

THE MYERS-BRIGGS SCALES ARE:

Extroverts (E) ◄———————————► **Introverts (I)**

This scale explores how people respond and interact with the outside world. People displaying high E traits are usually action-orientated and enjoy frequent social interaction whereas high I traits demonstrate thoughtful thinkers who enjoy solitude.

Sensors (S) ◄———————————► **Intuitors (N)**

This scale explores how people gather information from the outside world. People displaying high S traits focus on facts and details and enjoy hands-on experiences whereas high N traits pay more attention to patterns and impressions and enjoy speculating and imagining future possibilities.

Thinkers (T) ◄———————————► **Feelers (F)**

This scale explores how people make decisions from the information they gather. Those displaying high T traits place emphasis on facts and objective data and tend to be consistent, logical and objective when making decisions whereas those with a high F trait are subjective and consider people and emotions when making decisions.

Judges (J) ◄———————————► **Perceivers (P)**

This scale explores how people tend to deal with the outside world. Those with a high J trait prefer structure and order whereas those with a high P trait are more flexible.

In the MBTI there are four questions. Each question has two columns made up of a number of statements. The person is asked to choose which column best describes them. The responses indicate which end of the scale the individual's personality fits (E/I, S/N, T/F and J/P). These are then categorised into one of 16 personality types. For example, people with preferences for being *Extroverts, Sensors, Thinkers* and *Judges* are categorised as *ESTJ.*

HOW TO USE IT

By using the MBTI, you can gain an indication of where you and the person you are coaching stand on each of the four scales and can develop an appreciation as to whether your coaching style is compatible with the learning style of the individual. Here are a few tips to help you out with planning coaching that caters for people with each personality type:

Personality type	Will respond better by…
ESTJ	Being asked to follow directions to the letter.
ESTP	Learning about real things: sights, sounds and experiences.
ESFP	Trusting their instincts and abilities when solving problems.
ESFJ	Being in situations where things are certain or controlled.
ENFP	Not having to deal with routine and uninspiring tasks.
ENFJ	Speculating on how others may be affected.
ENTP	Generating new ideas and theories rather than detail.
ENTJ	Avoiding confrontation or heated discussion.
ISTJ	Working with clearly defined schedules and assignments.
ISTP	Learning and understanding how things work.
ISFP	Working on concrete information rather than abstract theories.
ISFJ	Sitting back and observing others.
INFP	Solving problems based on their personal values, not logic.
INFJ	Expressing themselves on paper.
INTP	Being encouraged to share their thoughts with others.
INTJ	Working by themselves rather than in groups.

Be aware that although an understanding of someone's personality may be helpful in predicting their behaviour it is not an entirely reliable forecast.

QUESTIONS TO ASK YOURSELF

■ What is my personality type?
■ Am I planning coaching that caters for people with certain personality types?

SECTION 2

UNDERSTAND WHAT MOTIVATES PEOPLE

INTRODUCTION

Motivation is an incredibly complex issue to get to grips with. Definitions will vary from it *being the thing you do to get others to do something* (extrinsic motivation) to *something that happens inside people that gets them to do something* (intrinsic motivation). I'm surprised by the lack of unanimity in defining a concept that is so important when it comes to coaching or managing people to become effective performers.

If you want to become a good coach, recognise that people will only be motivated to learn if they:

- accept they have a need to learn;
- believe they have the potential to learn;
- put learning as a priority.

Using this will be a valuable checklist when coaching someone. If there is a blockage at any of the three points, you need to address this as any further attempts at coaching may be futile. There are many different theories regarding motivation. In this section, I've chosen three famous theories on motivation which will help you to ensure the individual has the right level of motivation to want to learn.

Although there are differences in the three theories, the principles on which all three are based are that the people you are coaching will be more disposed to learn if:

- there are good facilities and equipment available for the coaching;
- the people being coached have a say in the design and delivery of the coaching;
- coaches are enthusiastic about the subject and act in an approachable but professional manner;
- coaches set challenging but realistic objectives;
- feedback is given in a positive and helpful manner.

Poor motivation may not just affect an individual's capacity to learn but may also contribute to any disruptive behaviour they may display (see Theories 26–28). Generate good motivation and you won't have to deal with behavioural issues.

THEORY 5 # JOHN KELLER: THE ARCS MODEL OF MOTIVATIONAL DESIGN

Use this when you want to generate interest and motivation on the part of the learner.

Keller claimed that his *ARCS model of motivational design* enables a coach to select coaching strategies that connect to coaching goals, while generating interest and motivation on the part of the learner. ARCS is an acronym for *attention*, *relevance*, *confidence* and *satisfaction*, which Keller asserts are the four variables that influence motivation.

THE KEY PARTS OF THE MODEL CAN BE SUMMARISED AS:

Attention: Someone's attention can be obtained in one of three ways: (a) perceptual arousal – a change in voice level, light intensity, environmental conditions or a surprising piece of information; (b) inquiry arousal – creating a problem which can only be resolved if the learner acquires new knowledge or skills; (c) variability – incorporating this will help prevent the learner becoming bored and tuning out.

Relevance: This emphasises the importance of someone understanding why they should expend effort on a given task. This can be achieved in one of three ways: (a) goal orientation – demonstrating how the new knowledge or skill will help them achieve present or future goals; (b) motive matching – understanding how someone's motive structure can lead to a conducive learning environment; (c) familiarity – people tend to be most interested when the content of coaching has some connection to past experiences.

Confidence: This highlights the importance of the person being coached believing they can succeed. This can be developed in one of three ways: (a) learning requirements – stipulating what's expected of them; (b) success opportunities – allowing people a few quick wins on tasks; (c) personal control – giving someone a sense of ownership of their development.

Satisfaction: This sums up someone's sense of self-worth after completing a task and can either take the form of: (a) natural consequences where they feel satisfaction at just acquiring new skills or knowledge; (b) positive consequences where they receive incentives in the form of money, promotion or special privileges as a result of applying new skills or knowledge.

Keller maintains that his model helps connect coaching to the goals of the person being coached, provides stimulation and offers appropriate levels of challenge.

HOW TO USE IT

Keller's ARCS model will provide you with a strategy for coaching that will be underpinned by a greater understanding of what makes a learner eager and willing to sit through the session, knowledge of how to keep the learner interested and make your sessions more appealing to both you and the learner. Here are a few tips on how to use the model:

- Firstly, you have to grab their attention. Do or say something that will make them sit up and listen. Starting off with a startling fact or statistic will often do the trick. Another approach might be to set them a challenging task or problem to solve. The important thing is that you get them curious and wanting to know more.

- Secondly, you need to show them how the content of the session is relevant to them. They need to know what's in it for them so tell them what they will be able to do by the end of the session and what impact this will have on them. Case studies that depict what others have achieved following coaching is a great technique to use here.

- Thirdly, having made absolutely certain that you haven't scared them off with ridiculous expectations of what they'll be able to do, you need to give them the confidence that they will be able to cope with what's expected of them. If they are struggling over any aspect of the coaching, let them know that you're not infallible and how you had to work hard to overcome problems.

- Finally, people will want acknowledgement for a task well done. Make sure that you provide appropriate feedback throughout, not just at the end, of the coaching session. It's important therefore that you commend them for effort as well as outcome. If people are satisfied at what they've achieved get them to think about what their next steps should be.

QUESTIONS TO ASK YOURSELF

- How well do I know the people who I am coaching?
- Have I designed the content of the session so that it's at the right level of understanding and challenge for them?

THEORY 6 DOUGLAS MCGREGOR: X AND Y THEORY

Use this when you want to know the right motivation technique to use with people.

McGregor's theory was originally used to categorise managers. The theory is based on a set of assumptions that represents an extreme vision of operating.

THEORY X MANAGERS BELIEVE THAT MOST PEOPLE:
will avoid putting in the effort whenever possible;
will need to be persuaded to perform;
have little ambition;
lack creativity.

THEORY Y MANAGERS BELIEVE THAT MOST PEOPLE:
want to put the effort in;
are eager to take responsibility for their work;
show ambition;
are creative.

Interpreting McGregor's ideas in terms of coaching would indicate that:

- **Theory X** coaches rely on coercion and external stimuli to promote a change in behaviour. They believe it is their responsibility to structure coaching and energise the people they are coaching.
- **Theory Y** coaches rely on the people they are coaching to have the inner desire to want to change their behaviour. They believe it is their responsibility to create the climate where self-motivated people will flourish.

In this interpretation, it is important to stress that not all *X-rated* coaches are bad and not all *Y-rated* coaches are good. There's room for both approaches, given the nature of the individuals they are working with and the context in which behaviour modification is taking place.

HOW TO USE IT

Now for some bad news: you will encounter some people who you manage or coach who would be in the category of X-rated; they are indifferent to learning and resist change (see Theories 26–28). If you are shocked by this, go straight to Kubler-Ross for advice (see Theory 72). Once you've gone through the *shock* and *anger* stages, you reach *bargaining*, where you have to decide whether to accept the situation and move on or do something about it. This might involve taking a hard line and excluding them from coaching sessions or negotiating terms on which you can either offer an external stimulus or ways that will improve their inner desire to want to change. It's important that whatever you choose to do you have the backing of your organisation. Here are some tips to help you:

- Theory X coaching is about command, control and fear. Your style here is about telling the person you are coaching what needs to be done and the implications of not doing it (see Theories 14–16).

- Theory Y coaching is about cooperation and good working relationships. Your style here is about suggesting ways of doing things and stimulating the person you are coaching to go ahead and do it themselves (see Theories 17–22).

Don't assume that it is always right to embrace Theory Y and disregard Theory X when you are coaching. You may have to consider adopting an approach that lies somewhere between the two extremes. Be careful if you do go for a hybrid approach that you are consistent, especially if you are coaching a group of people. Treating people differently in a group may lead to accusations of favouritism.

QUESTIONS TO ASK YOURSELF

- Do I consider myself to be a Theory X or Theory Y coach?
- Am I adopting an approach that takes into account the individual involved and the context in which the coaching is taking place?

THEORY 7 # FREDERICK HERZBERG: HYGIENE FACTORS AND KITAS

Use this when you want to understand the factors that lead to satisfaction and dissatisfaction at work and how to influence these.

Herzberg suggested that there are two factors that influence how satisfied or dissatisfied people are at work. He used the term *motivating factors* to describe the actions that create satisfaction and *hygiene factors* to describe the conditions that if they fall below acceptable levels create dissatisfaction. Examples of *motivating* factors include: achievement, recognition and responsibility. Examples of *hygiene* factors include: pay, working conditions and supervision.

Herzberg stresses the importance that the elimination of a dissatisfier will not automatically provide satisfaction. He uses the term *KITAs* (literally 'kicks in the derriere' – well not quite literally) to describe some ineffective motivational strategies.

THESE CAN BE SUMMARISED AS:

Negative physical KITAs: These include yelling, screaming, threatening and any other form of intimidation.

Negative psychological KITAs: These include more subtle forms of intimidation and include emotional game playing and other forms of psychological manipulation.

Herzberg argued that the single strongest motivator was achievement. He claimed that people are not motivated by fear of failure but they are motivated by a sense of achieving something and as a result being recognised for this.

HOW TO USE IT

Don't assume that if you, as a coach, eliminate a dissatisfier for the person you are coaching that you have created satisfaction – you have only eliminated dissatisfaction. For example, if the person you are coaching complains that you are not friendly enough towards them, smiling and cracking the odd joke may remove their dissatisfaction with your personality but according to Herzberg you will not have created a motivator. You need to be aware of the factors that really motivate people to want to learn. Here are some tips to help you with this:

- Make the coaching interesting by finding out the individual's learning style preference (see Theories 2–4). Set challenging but realistic learning objectives (see Theories 11–13). Remember that making them too challenging will result in demotivation but making them too easy will result in complacency. When they do achieve something as a result of your coaching, appreciate what they have achieved and share this appreciation with others in the team.

- Give positive feedback whenever possible. Never underestimate the value of the odd 'well done' or 'that was great'. It's amazing the impact that doing this publicly has on morale and productivity.

- Avoid using KITAs at all costs. Employment laws now frown on physical or psychological intimidation. Even if there were no such laws, using force or playing games with people's minds is hardly an ethical way of coaching someone.

QUESTIONS TO ASK YOURSELF

- How well do I understand the factors that motivate the people I am coaching?

- How good am I at appreciating the achievements of the people I am coaching?

SECTION 3

BE A GOOD COMMUNICATOR

INTRODUCTION

I once sat in a two-day session with someone coaching me and a group of others how to be effective managers. We were putting together a presentation on teamworking. We waited a good few minutes for him to say something. He just sat there. He sat there impassively all day saying nothing. We just got on with our presentation. We came back the second day and he just sat there. By mid-morning, we had a number of flip charts outlining our thoughts. We were pleased with what we had put together when our coach uttered, 'Mmm! more paper than process'. This shook us rigid and we began to question the ideas behind our presentation.

I also remember how, as a 21-year-old trainee teacher, I was so frustrated by my class's refusal to listen to what I was saying that I yelled out, 'You are the worst class I've ever taught!'. One of my class responded by telling me they'd heard that I'd told another group the same thing the day before. The only impact I created was to diminish my credibility and control over the class even further.

The point I am making here is that in order to be effective, communication has to have a clear message and be delivered in a manner that will create the most impact. Good communication can be linked to effective motivation in that it's about thought transmission, not information transmission: what it is you want them to understand, not what you want them to hear.

The theories covered in this section go from the very basic and possibly the most widely used communication model to two theories related to the state of mind that people are in when they give and receive messages. Using all three of these theories in tandem will, I promise you, make you a more effective communicator.

THEORY 8

MICHAEL ARGYLE: THE COMMUNICATION CYCLE MODEL

Use this when you want to avoid communication breakdowns.

Argyle maintained that communication was an essential tool that coaches needed to perfect in order to deliver effective teaching of any description. He asserts that it is a skill that can be developed. He suggests that this takes the form of a linear model in which there are six core components. The model can be depicted as follows:

Idea occurs ▸ Message coded ▸ Communication channel ▸ Message received ▸ Message decoded ▸ Message understood

THE CORE COMPONENTS RELATIVE TO COACHING CAN BE SUMMARISED AS:

Idea occurs: This is where the coach wants to try something out with the client that he feels will improve performance.

Message coded: The coach then has to decide what to say or do that will clarify what the idea is.

Communication channel: The coach has to determine which method of communication (verbal, written, demonstration) should be used to convey the message.

Message received: The coach has to seek confirmation that the message has been received.

Message decoded: The client has to break down and analyse what the message means. The coach has to ensure that the message has been decoded in an efficient and effective manner.

Message understood: The coach has to ensure that the client fully understands the message.

Variations on Argyle's model include a feedback loop from *message understood* to *initial idea*, making it more of a cyclical rather than a linear model.

HOW TO USE IT

Argyle's model is perhaps the simplest and most widely used of all communication models. It is based on the principles that you need a sender (the coach), a receiver (the person being coached), the message (what the coach wants to achieve), a method for sending the message – *directing* (Theories 14–16), *showing* (Theories 17–19), *facilitating* (Theories 20–22), *stimulating* (Theories 23–25) and confirmation that the message was received and understood. Where problems occur is when the communication is compromised by *physical*, *psychological* or *semantic* barriers. Here are a few tips for avoiding these:

- **Physical barriers**: These relate to the message simply not being heard or read clearly. This can be caused by external noise, lack of clarity in writing or equipment failure. Avoid coaching where there are distractions, make sure that verbal and written communication is clear and test out any equipment before coaching to make sure it functions correctly.

- **Psychological barriers**: These occur when there is a lack of respect or trust in the coaching relationship. Steven Covey has a wonderful metaphor of the *Emotional Bank Account* to describe this. This is where both parties make *deposits* in the form of good behaviour and keeping promises or *withdrawals* in the form of bad behaviour or breaking promises. Too many withdrawals will bankrupt the relationship. Stay in credit by listening to what the other person has to say, by being thoughtful and meeting their needs, fulfilling commitments and keeping promises.

- **Semantic barriers**: These are simply when you use language or meaning beyond the comprehension of the person being coached. How does this sound? *As the derivative referred to as the implied subject, having a predisposition for eternal abstinence from the impartation of knowledge to one's maternal predecessor is essential, relative to the vacuum induction of avian induced ovum.* See how long it takes you to work this out.

A good way of avoiding all of these barriers is to seek feedback from the person you are coaching. Make sure that they can hear and understand your message and won't challenge it on the grounds of lack of your credibility to coach.

QUESTIONS TO ASK YOURSELF

- Are there any distractions that will affect the coaching session?
- Are my instructions clear and legible?
- Am I staying in emotional credit with the person I am coaching?

THEORY 9   # ERIC BERNE: TRANSACTIONAL ANALYSIS

Use this when you want to understand how the state of mind that you are in will influence how well the communication works.

Berne suggested that the state of mind we are in when we communicate with people will influence how the other person receives, interprets or acts on the communication. He proposed five states of mind, or *ego states*, that people use when communicating. These can be represented as:

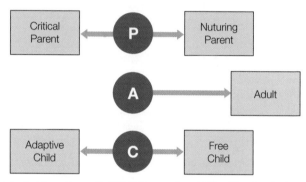

Source: Adapted from Berne, E. (1964) *Games People Play: The Psychology of Human Relationships*. London: Penguin.

THE *EGO STATES* CAN BE ADAPTED FOR COACHING AS FOLLOWS:

The Critical Parent state: This is where the coach is overbearing towards others and tells them what to do because they believe their way is the correct one.

The Nurturing Parent state: This is where the coach expresses concern for others and offers advice and support.

The Free Child state: This is where the coach is not afraid to share their feelings with others.

The Adaptive Child state: This is where the coach feels inhibited in expressing themselves in front of others.

The Adult state: This is where the coach acts by expressing themselves in a calm and rational manner.

Berne argues that, although behaving in the *Adult* state is generally the most effective coaching approach, there may be times when being in the *Parent* or even the *Child* state may get results.

HOW TO USE IT

I was working with middle managers in a major UK car manufacturing company. Karen, the only female manager in the group, told me that her line manager was making her life hell. She was constantly being undermined and talked to in a derisive manner. It was clear that her line manager had adopted a Critical Parent ego state. In order to comply, Karen had adopted an Adaptive Child ego state. This had resulted in the manager getting his way and Karen feeling despondent and unhappy in her work.

Using Berne's model, instead of lacking confidence and being anxious to please, she began to question: 'Why did he want her to do things?', 'How could they work together to tackle problems?', 'How could she support him to get things done?' She took the situation from 'Critical Parent addressing Adaptive Child' to 'adult addressing adult', and a much more satisfactory working relationship.

Here are a few tips if you are going to use Berne's model:

- Analyse what ego state you are in when dealing with another person (this could be any one of the five ego states).
- Recognise that you have the ability to adopt any ego state.
- Appreciate that:
  - *Parent* to *Child* or *Child* to *Parent* may get short-term results.
  - *Parent* to *Parent* may result in friction, especially if both are in *Critical Parent* mode.
  - *Child* to *Child* may result in inertia, especially if both are in *Adaptive Child* mode.
  - *Adult* to *Adult* is the best for long-term results.
- Start any interaction with words like 'How', 'What', 'When' and 'Why'. I promise you that this will get you to *Adult* to *Adult*. It may need perseverance but you will get there eventually.

This is a very powerful tool to have in your coaching toolbox. If you only pick a handful of theories to use as a coach, then pick this as one of them.

QUESTIONS TO ASK YOURSELF

- Am I sure that I am in the right frame of mind when I communicate with the person I am coaching?
- Do I appreciate what frame of mind they are in?
- Have I chosen the right ego state for the communication that will achieve a long-term satisfactory outcome?

THEORY 10   JOSEPH LUFT AND HARRY INGRAM: JOHARI WINDOWS

Use this when you want to assess how good you are as a coach in giving and receiving feedback.

Luft and Ingram suggested that by plotting the levels of your knowledge of self and knowledge held by others about you, you would have a greater understanding of effective communication. They claimed that the more open we are to others, and the more receptive we are with feedback from others, the better we will be able to communicate with them. They developed the *Johari* (taken from their first names) *window* as a means of depicting this. In the window frame there are four panes: The *Open Arena*, *Blindspot*, *Façade* and *Unknown* usually shown as:

The open arena	The blindspot
The façade	The unknown

Source: Luft, J. and Ingham, H. (1955) *The Johari Window: A Graphic Model of Interpersonal Awareness*. Proceedings of the Western Training Laboratory in Group Development. Los Angeles: UCLA Extension Office.

The size of the panes are determined by the extent of what is known by self and known by others.

EACH PANE CAN BE SUMMARISED AS:

The Open Arena: These are things known by self and by others.

The Blindspot: These are things not known by self but known by others.

The Façade: These are things known by self but not known by others.

The Unknown: These are things not known by self or by others.

Luft and Ingram devised a characteristic test to help people gauge the degree of what they know about themselves and how this correlates with what others know about them. They suggest that the responses can be mapped onto a grid that produces a window frame that will have unequal sized panes. The ideal frame for effective communication is where the *Open Arena* pane is the largest one.

HOW TO USE IT

As a coach, merely sharing information about yourself may not be sufficient to enlarge the *Open Arena* pane. You should be receptive to what the people you are coaching know or feel about you. This will reduce the size of the *Blindspot* pane but you need to embrace feedback from others without fear of humiliation. Here are some tips to help you as a coach to have a more open communication pane:

- Don't be afraid to ask for feedback. Make sure the people you are coaching know that you want this and care about what they have to say. Don't come over as a know-it-all and act on what they have to say. You may not always agree with what they have to say as long as you understand and respect what they are saying.

- Be willing to share things about yourself. Let the people you are coaching know what you are thinking. Making them aware of what you are thinking will help them to understand what you are trying to achieve with them.

- Be receptive to finding out more about yourself. The process of self-discovery is often ignored by coaches who look on coaching as a one-way process. This process becomes shared discovery when you work on things together with the person or people you are coaching. It's important to realise that you cannot change others or yourself when there is a lack of awareness about what needs changing. The processes of self-discovery and shared discovery will help you to deal with this.

I'm fascinated by how two blokes called Joe and Harry created something that has such wide application. Educationalists use it to analyse how good people are at giving and receiving feedback. It's even used in business as a form of psychometric test to assess how open people are.

QUESTIONS TO ASK YOURSELF

- What's preventing me from sharing my thoughts with others?
- How can I be more receptive to what others think about me?

SECTION 4

SET THE RIGHT OBJECTIVES

INTRODUCTION

Objective setting is the starting point and arguably the most important aspect of the coaching process. The process of setting an objective focuses attention, affects behaviour and therefore has a direct impact on performance. The more specific and measurable an objective is, the more effective it is likely to be in changing behaviour. Making goals achievable and relevant to the needs of the organisation as well as those of the individual will have a significant impact on the motivation of the person being coached. Having a timeline for completion also generates a sense of urgency to complete the task. This process is often referred to by the SMART acronym (*specific, measurable, achievable, realistic, and timely*). This acronym has been extended in recent years to include making objectives *exciting* and *rewarding* thus making them SMARTER objectives.

If we accept that coaches will be working with people on issues related to either knowledge, skills or feelings, we need a framework for objective setting that will ensure objectives are set at the right level and satisfy the notion of being SMARTER. In this section I have included theory that covers a hierarchy of learning objectives for knowledge, skills and feelings. These are referred to as the *learning domains*:

- Intellectual development is said to be the *cognitive* domain.
- Skills development is said to be the *psychomotive* domain.
- Feelings and emotional development is said to be the *affective* domain.

Within each of these domains there is a structure denoting levels of learning from the very basic to quite complex levels. This is often referred to as a *taxonomy*. An important aspect of a *taxonomy* is that each level should be mastered before progression to the next level is possible. For the purpose of demonstrating how to use each of the theories, for each entry, I'm going to use a learning experience that most adults will have undertaken – that of *learning to drive*. I will cover what, how and where to deliver and assess learning in each of the categories. See if you can adapt and adopt each of the *how to use* entries to suit the needs of the people who you are coaching.

THEORY 11 | # BENJAMIN BLOOM: LEVELS IN THE COGNITIVE DOMAIN

Use this to ensure the most appropriate level of support is offered to people to help them to develop their intellectual capacity.

Although Bloom made contributions to the development of taxonomies in all three learning domains, it was his work in the mid-1950s on learning in the cognitive domain that provided the basis for ideas for preparing learning objectives which have been developed and used by teachers, trainers and coaches throughout the world.

Bloom's taxonomy is based on a six-level structure which can be depicted as:

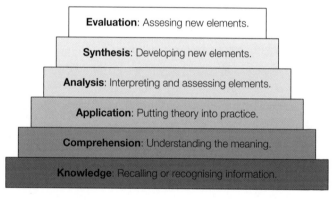

Evaluation: Assesing new elements.

Synthesis: Developing new elements.

Analysis: Interpreting and assessing elements.

Application: Putting theory into practice.

Comprehension: Understanding the meaning.

Knowledge: Recalling or recognising information.

Source: Bloom, B.S., Engelhart, M.D., Furst, E.J. *et al.* (1956) *Taxonomy of Educational Objectives: The Classification of Educational Goals. Handbook I: Cognitive Domain.* New York: David McKay Company.

Bloom argued that understanding and being able to apply knowledge was essential before higher levels of intellectual development could be reached.

HOW TO USE IT

Let's assume that you are coaching learner drivers in the knowledge they require to pass the driving test exam. Learner drivers will learn best about essential knowledge in a classroom. Here's how you can work through the levels:

- At the very basic level you want learner drivers to be able to recall facts from the Highway Code or recognise where controls are when asked. Simple questions and answers or multiple-choice questions will work well here.

- At the second level you want learner drivers to explain or interpret meaning from a given scenario. For example, ask them how they might recognise an accident has occurred or what happens if they try to change gears without depressing the clutch.

- Once they have demonstrated they know and understand facts, get the learner to use this knowledge and understanding in response to real-life circumstances. Give them a more complicated scenario related to driving and ask them how they would respond.

- Analysis and synthesis are the processes of breaking down the constituent parts of a concept and building up a new entity. This may be beyond the scope of learning to drive but looking for transferability of knowledge gained to other concepts would fall into this category.

This is probably the most straightforward of the domains in terms of planning, delivery and assessment. It actually requires no natural driving ability on behalf of the coach and coaching can be done online. Assessment is built on the answers to questions that are either correct or incorrect.

Now see if you can apply this in your own coaching context.

QUESTIONS TO ASK YOURSELF

- Have I determined at what level I need to set the objective?
- Have I agreed these with the person I am coaching?
- How will I know when we have reached the required level?

THEORY 12 | # RAVINDRAKUMAR DAVE: LEVELS IN THE PSYCHOMOTIVE DOMAIN

Use this to ensure the most appropriate level of support is offered to people to help them to develop their skills.

Of a number of taxonomies developed for the psychomotive domain, Dave's version in the late 1960s is the most prominent related to adult learning and the one that is most commonly referred to.

Dave's taxonomy is based on a five-level structure which can be depicted as:

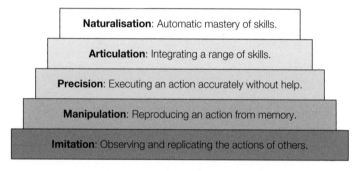

Naturalisation: Automatic mastery of skills.

Articulation: Integrating a range of skills.

Precision: Executing an action accurately without help.

Manipulation: Reproducing an action from memory.

Imitation: Observing and replicating the actions of others.

Source: Dave, R.H. (1970) 'Psychomotor levels' in Armstrong, R.J. (ed.) *Developing and Writing Behavioral Objectives*. Tuscon, AZ: Educational Innovators Press.

Dave argued that the ability to first observe and imitate skills, and then to replicate skills from memory, had to be mastered before higher levels of artistry could be achieved.

HOW TO USE IT

Let's assume that you are coaching learning drivers in the skills they require to pass the driving test. Learner drivers will learn best about essential skills in a car. Here's how you can work through the levels:

■ Start the process by demonstrating how to do various activities like depressing the clutch, changing gears etc. After each demonstration get the learner driver to copy what you did.

■ Once you are satisfied they can reproduce the activity correctly get them to do it from verbal instructions.

- Now get them to perform a range of activities with precision without assistance or instruction, for example moving through the gears or steering in a straight line.

- Take the learner driver out on the road and get them to adapt and integrate the range of activities into the process of driving to an acceptable standard.

- When they reach the stage of unconscious competence (they can do things with precision without having to think about it) then they will be ready to take the test.

- Be wary that the stage after unconscious competence is unconscious incompetence (they do the wrong things without being aware they are doing it wrong). Don't allow them to drift into this through complacency.

This is less straightforward than teaching in the cognitive domain as it requires the coach to be able to demonstrate skills and make judgements about performance that may be interpretive and not based on simple right or wrong assessments.

Now see if you can apply this in your own coaching context.

QUESTIONS TO ASK YOURSELF

- Have I determined at what level I need to set the objective?
- Have I agreed this with the person I am coaching?
- How will I know when we have reached the required level?

DAVID KRATHWOL AND BENJAMIN BLOOM: LEVELS IN THE AFFECTIVE DOMAIN

Use this when you want to ensure the most appropriate level of support is offered to people to help them to develop their feelings and emotions.

Krathwol and Bloom suggested a structure for developing attitudes and feelings. They produced a five-level model, usually depicted as:

Internalise: To adopt a new belief system.

Conceptualise: To reconcile internal conflicts with existing values.

Value: To attach meaning to the learning and express personal views.

Respond: To react to and participate in a learning activity.

Receive: To have a willingness to be open to the learning experience.

Source: Krathwol, D., Bloom, B.S. and Masia, B.B. (1973) *Taxonomy of Educational Objectives: The Classification of Educational Goals. Handbook II: Affective Domain*. New York: David McKay Company.

Krathwol and Bloom argued that a willingness to be receptive to challenging feelings and emotions, and a genuine desire to want to change, were essential elements of this model.

This is probably the most difficult of the three domains for the majority of coaches to feel really comfortable in. It is more complex than the other two taxonomies with differences in levels more subtle, especially between levels 3, 4 and 5.

HOW TO USE IT

Let's assume that you are coaching learning drivers to overcome the fears or emotional barriers they have regarding driving. Learner drivers will learn best about emotions and feelings somewhere quiet away from the vehicle and teaching classroom. Here's how you can work through the levels:

- Start by finding a suitable spot where you can get the learner to discuss any problems they have with learning to drive, psychological as well as physical. This could be a one-to-one session or in small groups; wherever the learner feels comfortable.

- Establish a rapport with the learner by talking to them about issues other than driving.
- Get them to explore the issues causing problems with their driving and why it's inhibiting their capacity to learn. Don't get too immersed in issues beyond your understanding. If the extent of the physical and psychological problems is beyond your scope, then refer them to specialist advisers.
- If they can qualify and quantify their beliefs then get them to reflect on what they can do about them.
- Avoid giving them the answer to their problems: get them to sort them out for themselves.

The application of this model for coaching learner drivers isn't apparent at first glance. It's only when you start to get into it that you begin to appreciate its application. This could involve the coach examining the learner driver's fears about driving or a lack of concern about other road users. It will require value judgements that may have no right or wrong answers.

Now see if you can apply this in your own coaching context.

QUESTIONS TO ASK YOURSELF

- Have I determined at what level I need to set the objective?
- Have I agreed this with the person I am coaching?
- How will I know when we have reached the required level?

SECTION 5

COACHING THROUGH DIRECTING

INTRODUCTION

irecting and telling others what to do is a behaviourist approach, based on the principle of stimulus and response. It is a coach-led activity which assumes the coach is in control of what needs to be done, how it will be done and what evidence of behavioural change needs to be produced. The basic premise of behaviourism is that people need to be directed and that if the stimulus is something that the individual wants (a reward) or fears (a punishment) then they will respond accordingly and there will be a noticeable change in behaviour.

The theory is rooted in the late nineteenth-century studies into how people behave and the emergence of the discipline of psychology. Many of the principles that underpin behaviourism were developed from psychologists working with animals and then transferring their theories to human beings.

Although some of the theory was determined through research that may these days be considered unethical, behaviourism remained the basis of teaching approaches throughout the twentieth century and is still useful when working with less mature learners or on subjects where precise adherence to procedures is essential and in environments where there are health hazards. Behaviourism is not without its critics, however, who view it as an autocratic, transmission-led approach which fails to recognise the independent and enquiring nature of people.

I've chosen three theories for this section from the behaviourist school of learning. Two are classical behaviourism and the third is a contemporary look at the impact of telling people what to do. The coach's role in all three respects is about being in control and directing the person being coached.

THEORY 14   IVAN PAVLOV: CLASSICAL CONDITIONING

Use this when you want to reduce people's negative feelings towards a subject.

Pavlov's contribution to our understanding of how people learn stems from his work as a physiologist and his research into the digestive secretions of dogs, for which he was awarded the Nobel Prize in 1904.

His research indicated that presenting a dog with food (an *unconditioned stimulus*) can provoke a reflex action in the form of the dog salivating (an *unconditioned response*). Add an accompaniment to the stimulus (ringing a bell) and after a period of time remove the original stimulus (the food) and the dog will salivate just at the sound of the bell. He referred to this phenomenon as a *conditioned response* because the dog had been taught to associate food with the sound of the bell ringing.

In later experiments Pavlov discovered that the conditioned response would disappear if the dog eventually realised that food was not automatically served with the ringing of the bell. He used the term *classical conditioning* to describe this. The principle of *classical conditioning* marked a ground-breaking step in establishing psychology as a scientific discipline and influenced the work of other behaviourist psychologists.

HOW TO USE IT

As a coach, you will find that there may on occasions be reluctance on the part of the person you are coaching to respond to what you need to achieve with them. This may be simply because the individual is an unwilling participant in the exercise (see Theories 5–7) or they have a genuine fear of the subject. There is a whole raft of subject negativity or phobias that can be addressed by removing someone's negative responses to the subject. Here are some tips on how to do this:

- Firstly, getting the individual to examine the root cause of their negative feelings towards the subject before making them aware of the relevance of the subject to them.

- Try taking out some of the menace about failing tests in the subject by giving some easy tasks where the individual can achieve a few successes before building up the intensity of the tasks gradually.

- Finally, make sure that you are generous in your praise when they complete a task. By doing this, you will condition people to look forward to the subject.

Let's be clear here you are unlikely to turn someone with a dread of maths into a Bertrand Russell or even a Carol Vorderman overnight, but you can at least work with someone to help them overcome their fear of the subject.

QUESTIONS TO ASK YOURSELF

- How well have I got my client to examine the root cause of their negativity to the subject?
- Have I provided sufficient stimulus to get them to address this negativity?

THEORY 15 # EDWIN GUTHRIE: CONTIGUITY THEORY

Use this when you want to replace someone's bad habits with good ones.

Although Guthrie was a behaviourist in the classical traditional mode, he rejected the notion of other behaviourists that conditioning needed reinforcement (positive or negative) to be successful. He argued instead that once you have been successful from a course of action, you will habitually repeat that action expecting the same outcome until something happens to create a different response. He referred to this as *contiguity theory*.

Guthrie suggests that you can't break a person's bad habits but you can replace them with good ones.

THIS CAN BE DONE BY:

The threshold method: Begin by reducing the level of stimulus so that the negative response to the stimulus hardly seems worth it to the individual.

The exhaustion method: Keep presenting the stimulus until the individual reaches 'fatigue' level at which stage they will lose the desire to act badly and change from negative to positive response.

The incompatibility method: Present a stimulus that produces a behaviour that is incompatible with the undesired behaviour.

In a behaviour modification context, Guthrie advocated that when working with groups, the coach should focus on what the individual does rather than what the group does as a whole. In this respect, he argues that average group behaviour may not represent the type of behaviour found in individuals.

HOW TO USE IT

Let me tell you a true story.

Some years ago I was being pestered by a couple of young lads who each night around about 7 o'clock would play their music too loud outside my house. When I told them to lower the volume they ignored me. The next night, I asked them politely to lower the volume, they still ignored me. After a week of this, I told them that I was beginning to enjoy their music and offered them £2 to come back the following night. They came back, played their music and I offered them £1 to come back the following night. They moaned that this was half what I'd paid them previously but still came back. This time I told them to come back but I couldn't afford to pay them anything. One of the lads said, 'if you think we're going to do this for nothing...' and walked off chuntering. I never saw them again.

What I did was to replace their intrinsic desire to want to annoy someone with an external stimulus (the money). Using Guthrie's *threshold* method, I reduced the level of stimulus to the point where the stimulus no longer had the desired effect and the motivation to act as they did disappeared. I could have used the *exhaustion* method and simply ignored them till they got fed up and went off to annoy someone else but I couldn't be sure how long this would take. I suppose I could have used the *incompatibility* method and played my AC/DC vinyls at full blast till they couldn't hear themselves think. I'm not sure how my neighbours would have reacted to this and the thought of getting an ASBO at my age put me off doing this.

Think about how, as a coach, you can apply Guthrie's theory to dealing with someone's bad habits, whatever they may be. Whichever method you then adopt depends on the issue that you have to deal with and how long you have to resolve it.

Now for a confession: I made that story up. I felt that, if you thought it was a true story you might read it (my *X-rated* instincts). I should have believed you would read it anyway because of your inner desire to want to learn as much as possible (my *Y-rated* instincts). (If you want to know more about X and Y rated instincts see Theory 6.)

QUESTIONS TO ASK YOURSELF

▓ How well have I gauged the extent of my client's bad habits?

▓ Have I chosen the right method to get them to address this?

ROBERT MERTON: SELF-FULFILLING PROPHECY

Use this when you want to influence the person you are coaching to believe in themselves.

Although examples of the *self-fulfilling prophecy* can be found in literature as far back as the ancient civilisations in Greece, China and India, it was Merton who first coined the phrase in the 1950s. He described it as an unfounded prediction that directly or indirectly has an impact on others and causes the prediction to become true. In other words, once people convince themselves that something is true, regardless of whether it is or not, they will act on that belief.

Merton applies his theory to analyse what happened in a fictitious bank run. This is a summary of the story he tells:

> The Last National Bank is a typical bank with some liquid assets but with most of the assets invested in other ventures. One day the bank has a large number of customers wanting to make withdrawals. Rumours spread that the bank is in financial difficulties and more customers flock to the bank. Eventually the scale of withdrawals exceeds the liquid assets held causing the bank to become insolvent. The rumours although unfounded had become a reality.

Merton suggests that the only way to break the cycle of self-fulfilling prophecy is by redefining the assumptions on which the original was based. In the case of the bank, he suggests that this would involve an early and positive statement or gesture to end rumours at the earliest possible stage.

Relating the theory to coaching, Merton argued that people who tend to be caught up in negative self-fulfilling prophecies often suffer from low self-esteem where they act on an overly critical evaluation of their performance. This leads to a tendency to have a pessimistic view of the world and their ability to influence their own situation for the better.

HOW TO USE IT

Here's a story of three characters in desperate need for some positive thinking:

How can you turn a coward into a hero, a dullard into a genius or an emotional vacuum into a great lover? That's exactly the challenge facing the coach (masquerading as a wizard) in Frank Baum's immortal story of *The Wizard of Oz*. He gave the Cowardly Lion a medal for courage, the Scatterbrain Scarecrow a diploma in education and the Tin Man a ticking clock (well Christian Barnard hadn't perfected heart transplants at this stage). If you don't know the results see the film; it's a classic.

Never underestimate the effect that you have on the people you are coaching. You exert enormous power over their lives and, through your attitude towards them, can turn them into successes or failures. Tell them they are doomed to fail and they may begin to accept failure as an inevitable consequence. Here are some tips about how you can apply the self-fulfilling prophecy to good effect:

- Give the people you are coaching a few tasks that are relatively easy to complete. Acknowledge their achievement of the task. A simple 'well done' or celebrating the achievement with others will do.
- Reward effort as well as achievement. Make sure individuals see the connection between effort and success.
- Get them to share what they have learned with others in the team. Develop a rapport among members of the team, whereby they acknowledge the efforts and successes of others. Simple nods of appreciation or a round of applause may be appropriate.
- Teach the people you are coaching how to handle the failures that inevitably they will experience from time to time. Support them to learn from mistakes as well as successes.

The Wizard's approach was simple. He had the power to destroy each of the people seeking his help but, by telling them they were brave/brainy/emotional, he made them believe in themselves and they gained the qualities they were seeking.

QUESTIONS TO ASK YOURSELF

- What can I tell the person I am coaching to give them self-belief?
- How can I do this without making them over-confident or arrogant?

SECTION 6

COACHING THROUGH FACILITATING

INTRODUCTION

Accepting that you are not in total control of the coaching process and that other people have a valuable contribution to make is a key principle in *humanism*. This is based on the belief that the individual is self-determining and free to make their own choices. It is a person-centred activity in which the individual plays an active role in deciding what role they should play in determining what they should be allowed to learn.

The basic premise of humanism is that people have a natural potential for learning and that significant learning takes place when the individual can see that the subject matter is relevant to them. In this situation, the coach acts as a facilitator; encouraging learning rather than identifying specific methods or techniques of instruction.

Although roots of the humanist movement can be traced back into religion and philosophy, it was the work of Montessori and Neill at the beginning of the twentieth century, that popularised the movement in education. The theory wasn't further developed until the early 1940s. It was popularised throughout the 1960s and 1970s as a result of a group of psychologists questioning the virtue of the behaviourist approach, which they felt portrayed a negative view of the person's capacity for self-determination, and the cognitivist approach which they argued was too obsessed with meaning and understanding.

As the movement grew to empower more people in making decisions about issues that affect their lives, so the emphasis switched from coach-centred to person-centred learning. Supporters of the humanistic approach argue that people appreciate not being evaluated or judged and relish the opportunity for their thoughts to be understood. Critics claim that not everyone seeks empowerment or feels comfortable when empowered, arguing that some people clearly want to be instructed in what to do.

I've chosen three theories in this section that include arguably the two most influential humanists (Maslow and Rogers) and a more contemporary addition to the humanist movement (Mezirow). The coach's role in all three respects is about releasing control and supporting the person being coached to take some ownership of the process.

THEORY 17 ABRAHAM MASLOW: HIERARCHY OF NEEDS

Use this when you want to understand the needs of the people that you are working with.

Maslow is best known for his studies into motivation. His most famous work was the 'hierarchy of needs' in which an individual's response to learning is dominated at any given moment by whichever need has priority.

The hierarchy of needs is divided into two phases. The two lower order needs relate to the physiological and safety aspects of learning (physical and psychological safety). Progression to the higher level is not possible unless lower level needs have been met. This is usually represented as a pyramid or series of steps:

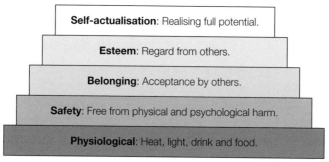

Self-actualisation: Realising full potential.

Esteem: Regard from others.

Belonging: Acceptance by others.

Safety: Free from physical and psychological harm.

Physiological: Heat, light, drink and food.

Source: Maslow, A.H. (1943) 'A theory of human motivation', *Psychological Review* 50(4), pp. 370–96.

Maslow suggests that few people experience self-actualisation in its full sense but many enjoy periods of 'peak experience' where they derive a great sense of achievement at mastering a skill or analysing a piece of information.

Maslow argues that although the motivation to progress through each level can be driven through either extrinsic or intrinsic forces, it is the inner desire to want to achieve (intrinsic motivation) that is important in the humanistic approach.

HOW TO USE IT

Don't feel that it is down to you as their coach to ensure that everyone's needs must be fully met. People can, and do, function in various states of contentedness. They also have expectations from you as their coach that, although conditions may not always be perfect, they should at the very minimum be tolerable. The following is an attempt to demonstrate how a person's needs can be met, partially if not fully:

- People will want to feel comfortable in the session, so make sure lighting, heating and ventilating systems are functioning properly. Build in drink and toilet breaks. Arrange seating according to the needs of the person/people who you are coaching.

- They will want to feel safe from physical and psychological harm, so make sure that you deal with threatening behaviour from any members of the group in an appropriate manner (see Theories 26–28) and if you are coaching a group, treat all members of the group fairly in a positive non-threatening manner.

- People will want to feel accepted by both the coach and their peers, so show them that you care for them and promote group interaction. Take time out to find out about their interests and mix members of the group up in practical activities.

- They will also want to feel a sense of pride in their achievements, so encourage them to come up with new ideas and original solutions to problems. Praise from you is good but praise from their peers is even better so get them to share their ideas with the rest of the group.

- Finally, people will want to feel that they have been coached to reach their full potential. You may have to be realistic, as their coach, about what you can achieve here. Don't be skimpy when it comes to celebrating success but make sure that you celebrate effort as well.

Understanding people's needs and having the right approaches to dealing with these needs will say a great deal about you, not just as a coach but as a person.

QUESTIONS TO ASK YOURSELF

- Am I creating the right conditions for coaching to be effective?
- How well am I making the people I am coaching feel about themselves?

THEORY 18　CARL ROGERS: FACILITATION

Use this to develop your skills as a facilitator coach.

Rogers was a driving force in the humanist movement, advocating a shift in emphasis in the learning process away from the teacher/coach towards the individual. This shift entailed the coach's role changing from one of authority, expertise and providing solutions, to one of facilitating the process of individuals arriving at their own solutions.

Rogers identified three elements which he felt were an important part of effective facilitation:

He described the main characteristics of these elements as:

- **Congruence**: having a sense of genuineness and honesty.
- **Empathy**: being able to understand the other person's emotions.
- **Respect**: demonstrating positive regard towards the other person.

Rogers's belief in his inability to teach anyone anything, merely to provide an environment conducive to effective learning, is the guiding principle of his theory.

HOW TO USE IT

Using facilitation as a coaching method is more about how you practise, than what you practise. It's about making the process of learning easier for people. In order to use this approach you must have a firm belief in your role as the facilitator, not the controller or director. Do this half-heartedly and you will not be adopting a humanistic approach. It's important therefore to look at the behaviours and actions necessary for good facilitation:

Behaviours

- Be true to yourself and don't be afraid to express your feelings.
- Be willing to consider issues from the other person's standpoint.
- Accept others for what they are in a non-critical and non-judgemental manner.

Actions

- Start by setting the mood and climate for the coaching session. How you come over to others in the opening stanza of the session will have a significant impact on how they perform during the session.
- Find out what the people you are coaching are expecting from the session. Get full agreement on what the learning outcomes will be. Write these down (this will be useful to refer to during the session).
- Have a range of learning resources available (exercises, tasks etc.).
- Act as a flexible resource to be utilised by the others and don't be afraid to become a learning participant.
- Find out what others gained from the session.
- Be willing to share your own feelings about the learning experience.
- Be receptive to criticism and never be afraid to recognise and accept your own limitations.

The behaviours and actions you display during a session will often stimulate other people's desire to want to learn more about the subject than the actual content of the session.

QUESTIONS TO ASK YOURSELF

- Am I being too reluctant in expressing my feelings about the performance of the people I am coaching?
- Am I considering issues from their standpoint?
- Am I being too judgemental about their values and beliefs?

THEORY 19   JACK MEZIROW:
             TRANSFORMATIONAL LEARNING

Use this when you want to induce more far-reaching change in people.

Mezirow suggested that transformational learning would induce more far-reaching behavioural change in the person and produce a more significant impact, or paradigm shift, than other kinds of learning.

He developed the concepts of *meaning perspectives*; an individual's overall view of the world and *meaning schemes*; smaller bits of knowledge and values relating to the individual's experiences. He argued that meaning perspectives change as a result of responses to life experiences, and provide the raw material for the changes that occur in transformational learning. Mezirow's theory of transformational learning is based on three main themes that can be represented as follows:

THE THREE THEMES CAN BE SUMMARISED AS:

Experience of life: provides the essential starting point in any coaching event.

Critical reflection: is the distinguishing feature of adult learning and the mechanism by which the person being coached questions the validity of their beliefs and values.

Rational discourse: induces the person being coached to explore the depth and meaning of their beliefs and values and to share these with their coach and peers.

Mezirow felt that the combination of reflection and discourse encouraged the person being coached to transform their views on life to be more inclusive which would in turn lead to greater interdependency and compassion for others.

HOW TO USE IT

Let's be honest, not all coaches are predisposed to engage in transformational learning, not all coaching situations lend themselves to this kind of experience and not all people being coached will feel comfortable being challenged over their values and beliefs. There will however be circumstances in the most unlikely situations when you may feel it is your responsibility to challenge unacceptable behaviour. A classic example of this is when someone you are coaching makes racist or sexist comments during a coaching session. Do you treat this in a passive or active manner?

Here are some important points to help you deal with this situation:

- If you decide to create a transformational learning environment with someone, it must be free from coercion. Never impose your views on others.
- Encourage people to critically reflect on, and discuss their beliefs openly.
- Have a commitment from all concerned (including yourself) to search for common ground or a synthesis of different points of view.
- Look for different ways to stimulate transformational learning such as sharing experiences, metaphors, role plays and case studies.
- Once the person realises that their old patterns of thinking are giving way to new patterns, support them to embed these patterns into their values and beliefs.

Always question yourself: what rights do I have to engage in transformational learning? If you can't answer this in the positive then don't do it.

QUESTIONS TO ASK YOURSELF

- Am I trying to force my values and beliefs on the person being coached?
- Am I encouraging the person being coached to learn from their mistakes as well as exploring elements of their successes?
- Am I helping the person being coached to examine assumptions and beliefs that may be hindering their performance?

SECTION 7

COACHING THROUGH SHOWING OTHERS HOW TO DO IT

INTRODUCTION

Working with someone on how to adapt and adopt what you have shown them is referred to as *cognitivism* and is based on the principle that information is actively processed inside the mind of the person and that learning takes place by searching for the relationships that exist between the various bits of information.

The basic premise is that learning is a process of gathering all of the relevant pieces of information together until they begin to form a complete picture. The analogy with a jigsaw can be drawn in which each individual piece has little meaning until connected with other pieces and a picture begins to emerge.

Cognitivist theory grew out of dissatisfaction with the behaviourist approach where the staunchest critics felt it was too focused on achieving a specific outcome and not on developing the individual's potential. There are many branches within cognitivism, such as constructivism and connectivism, which some would argue are separate theories in their own right. My stance in this section is to treat these as variations on the main theme of cognitivism.

As the need grew within teaching and coaching to promote people who were capable of deeper understanding and reasoned thinking, cognitivism became a new trend in thinking. Critics of the cognitive approach argue that it is too focused on personal developmental encounters rather than learning outcomes and that not all people have either the capacity, or the desire, to want to spend a vast amount of time processing information.

Cognitivism is probably one of the most difficult of the theories covered so far to understand. The basis of the three theories covered in this section are that people will learn through greater insight into problems and use techniques such as trial and error or role modelling to solve these problems themselves. The coach's role in all three respects is about showing the person being coached how to go about using these techniques but leaving them to work it out for themselves.

THEORY 20
THE GESTALTISTS: INSIGHT THEORY

Use this when the person being coached is struggling to develop a solution to a problem.

Wolfgang Kohler, Kurt Koffka and Max Wortheimer were the founders of the Gestalt movement in Germany in the 1920s. The word *Gestalt* means both 'pattern' and 'organised whole'. The basic principle behind Gestalt theory is that concepts such as *perception*, *learning*, *understanding* and *thinking* should be considered as interacting relationships combining together to form *insight* as depicted below:

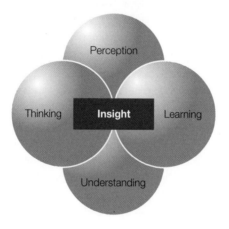

It is through this interaction that the Gestaltists claim that people have a flash of inspiration when trying to formulate solutions to a problem.

Although critics of gestaltism argue that the solution to a problem may be as a result of past experience of dealing with the problem rather than a flash of inspiration, many practitioners appreciate that people are capable of mentally organising the components of a problem and developing insightful solutions. People's reactions when 'the penny (or *pfennig*!) drops' can be rewarding for both you as the coach as well as the people being coached.

HOW TO USE IT

Although some say they're not in the same league as *Gorillas in the Mist*, the *Planet of the Apes* films are watchable. There is a great scene in *Origin of the Planet of the Apes* where the ape speaks its first coherent word and changes the balance of power in the primate world from humans to apes.

Why am I wittering on about apes? Well, it was through their study of apes trying to solve problems that the Gestaltists developed their theory of *learning through insight*. They observed that apes could actively perceive several possible solutions before finding the best answer. They referred to this as *insight*, a *discovery of thought* or *flash of brilliance*. This was different from the process of trial and error where the solution was reached by doing.

Trying to tell you how to use this theory would be defeating the object. You cannot coach people to be insightful, merely create the conditions in which insight is allowed to flourish. As a coach, do this by using the LEAP method:

■ **L**et people have the freedom to be risk takers.
■ **E**ncourage them to try new ideas.
■ **A**llow them not to be bound by too much emphasis on covering content.
■ **P**rovide them with time to reflect on what they've learned.

I can't resist using the example of Olympic gold medallist, Dick Fosbury. If his high jump coach had told him that the idea of jumping over the bar backwards was ludicrous, then high jumpers would still be using the straddle or scissor-kick methods and jumping well below the levels that are currently achieved.

QUESTIONS TO ASK YOURSELF

■ Am I allowing people to have sufficient freedom to take risks?
■ Am I supporting them to learn from any mistakes they make?

THEORY 21 # KARL PRIBRAM, GEORGE MILLER AND EUGENE GALLANTER: TEST-OPERATE-TEST-EXIT (TOTE)

Use this when you want a process for testing the effectiveness of an idea.

Pribram, Miller and Gallanter developed the TOTE model as a type of trial and error process, whereby someone adopts a course of action, tests its results and, if successful, makes adjustments until the ultimate outcome is achieved or chooses to exit the process. The process can be depicted as:

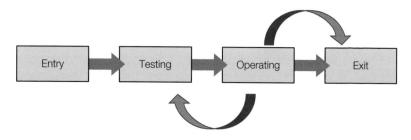

EACH ELEMENT IN THE PROCESS CAN BE SUMMARISED AS FOLLOWS:

Entry is the point at which you realise that you need to make changes to your present state.

Testing allows you to compare your present state with the desired one.

Operating is where you take action to make any adjustments necessary to work towards the desired state. This will create a new present state. If the new present state matches the desired one, you may exit the process. If not, you have to go back to testing.

Exit is when you have reached the desired state.

Pribram, Miller and Gallanter explain that an important part of the process is to record what takes part in each stage of the process and to appreciate that there may have to be several loops between *testing* and *operating* before the desired state can be reached (hence the acronym TOTE).

HOW TO USE IT

There's nothing complicated about coaching someone to use the TOTE. process. It's a process that we go through a dozen if not more times each day. If you want to achieve something, you behave in a manner designed to achieve that goal. You then test to see whether you have achieved it. If you are successful, end of story, if not try something different.

> When I was studying maths at university in the 1970s, I became fascinated by Fermat's Theorem. I won't bore you with the details of the theorem, but it was one of those conundrums that beset not just mathematics but life as well: where you know something to be true but can't prove it. Like many mathematicians, seduced by the offer of $100,000 to anyone who could prove the theorem, I spent the next 25 years dabbling with possible answers. My problem was that although I was following the structure set down in TOTE, my basic testing procedure was flawed. I was using trial-and-error when I should have been using logical deduction. When Andrew Wiles came up with his ground-breaking proof in 1993, he too found that he'd made a mistake and it was two years later, in conjunction with Richard Taylor, that he finally cracked it, just in time to claim his $100,000.

It's important when you are using a process like TOTE that you remember that even the simplest of processes fail if there are flaws in any operation within the process. Make absolutely certain therefore that when you apply a test it is valid and reliable and only exit the process when you are confident that the desired state has been reached.

QUESTIONS TO ASK YOURSELF

■ Am I being clear about what it is that's being tested and why it's being tested?

■ Am I making sure the person being coached doesn't exit the process until the desired state has been reached?

THEORY 22 # ALBERT BANDURA: ROLE MODELLING

Use this to promote the use of role modelling and peer coaching.

Bandura suggests that people modify their behaviour through observing others more so than through rewards or punishment. The observational process is underpinned by the notion that behaviour modification is achieved by observing the actions of others, mentally rehearsing whether these actions are appropriate and then initiating behaviour that was considered appropriate.

He based his theory on experiments conducted with two groups of children. One group witnessed scenes of adults physically and verbally attacking an inflatable doll. The other group witnessed scenes of adults caressing and talking affectionately to the doll. In both instances, when left alone, the groups imitated the behaviour of the adults who they had observed.

In order for someone to successfully imitate the behaviour of a role model, Bandura put forward a number of strategies.

BANDURA SUGGESTED THE INDIVIDUAL MUST BE ENCOURAGED TO:
pay attention to the behaviour;
remember what was seen or heard;
have the capacity to reproduce the behaviour;
have the motivation to want to reproduce it.

Bandura argued that people would be more receptive to modelling good behaviours if they believed that they were capable of executing the behaviour. He used the term *self-efficacy* to describe this. He suggested that observing their peers, rather than celebrities, would support an individual's belief in their capacity to execute the behaviour.

HOW TO USE IT

As a coach, using role models and peer coaching to demonstrate what behaviour is acceptable or unacceptable from the person who you are working with is a great technique. This will work of course if the person being coached has the same perception of the person being modelled as you have.

San Patrignano is a village in eastern Italy. Just over 1,300 people live there. What is unusual about the village is that over 80 per cent of its residents are rehabilitating drug addicts. When I visited the village, I was amazed to find that there is no formal policing and hardly any crime. Law and order is maintained through a process of role modelling in which former addicts work on a one-to-one basis with new residents demonstrating the type of behaviours that will help end their addiction. Since its inception in 1978 with a handful of addicts living in a communal house, the village now has 250 employees, 100 volunteers, a school, hospital, restaurants and Italy's fourth best-rated pizzeria.

Here are some important points to bear in mind if you want to use role modelling or peer coaching:

- Others will learn a great deal simply by observing good role models. As a coach, therefore, you must model appropriate behaviours and avoid modelling inappropriate behaviours such as making racist or sexist comments or bad punctuality.

- Describe the consequences of good behaviour as this will increase appropriate behaviour. Conversely, if you describe the consequences of bad behaviour this will decrease inappropriate behaviour.

- Don't expose others to a variety of role models who are stereotypes as this will only reinforce people's stereotypical notions of what's right or wrong.

- Make sure that others have realistic expectations of what they will achieve through modelling appropriate behaviours and believe that they are capable of modelling the new behaviour.

- Get the person you are coaching to think about people who have had an impact on their life. Ask them to choose maybe two or three who had a positive impact and the same number who had a negative impact. Get them to explore what it was that made them a good role model and what aspects of their behaviour they would want to emulate and what made them a bad role model and what aspects of their behaviour they would want to avoid.

QUESTIONS TO ASK YOURSELF

- Am I being a positive role model for the people I am coaching?
- Where can I find peers for the person being coached to use as good role models?

SECTION 8

COACHING THROUGH STIMULATING

INTRODUCTION

I have referred to the theories in this section as coming under the heading of *neurolism*. Don't go rushing to the dictionary or try *googling* this term. It doesn't exist. It is a term that I have adopted to cover the phenomena known as *brain-based learning* or *information processing theory*.

As the three main theories covered so far in this part were developed during the early to mid part of the twentieth century, I wanted to include a section that gave learning a slightly different perspective and builds on the cognitive branch of teaching and learning.

Neurolism draws on research conducted by neuroscientists and neuro-physiologists. The basis of *neurolism* therefore is the anatomy of the brain and its capacity to cope with complex phenomena such as emotions, intelligence, thinking and learning. In order to make sense of the entries that follow, think of the brain in terms of a computer and the way that it processes information. If we adopt this metaphor, we see that incoming information is acted upon by a series of processing systems. Each of these systems accepts, rejects or transforms the information in some way, resulting in some form of a response.

Where there is a difference between the rhetoric of the metaphor and the reality of the brain is in the type of processing of which each is capable. Computers are only capable of processing one bit of information at a time before moving on to the next bit, whereas the brain often engages in a multitude of bits of information simultaneously. There is also an issue about predictability with the computer always reacting to the same input in exactly the same manner, whereas the brain may be subjected to emotional or environmental pressures that cause differences in reactions. Differences apart, there are similarities in terms of *reception*, *perception* and *retention* that are important to our understanding of the theory and that I want to explore during this section.

THEORY 23 DONALD HEBB: ASSOCIATIVE LEARNING

Use this when you want to investigate issues related to learning and memory.

Hebb formulated a theory to explain what takes place during the process of associative learning. He argued that this happens when nerve cells in the brain are simultaneously and repeatedly active, creating the synapses (or links) that lead to cell assemblies. A theory that is often referred to as *cells that fire together, wire together*.

He suggested that the associative process was more noticeable in childhood learning when new cell assemblies are being formed. He uses the example of a baby hearing footsteps (*audio assemblies*), then seeing a face (*visual assemblies*) and being picked up (*tactile assemblies*) to describe how the process works. This can be depicted as:

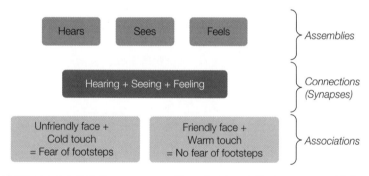

Hebb argued that the process of learning in adults is more sophisticated than in children and involves the rearrangement of existing cell assemblies rather than the creation of new ones.

HOW TO USE IT

Okay, we're not neuroscientists and the study of how the brain functions is incredibly complex. Understanding how to apply Hebb's theories as a coach is based on the principle that learning affects the brain in two different ways: it creates brand new synapses (links) or rearranges existing ones. Either way, the brain is remoulded to take in new data and, if it is useful, retains it.

To use Hebb's theory effectively as a coach, keep the following tips in mind:

- Accept that people learn differently. Some will have more connections and interconnections than others and will have a more developed organised knowledge structure and therefore be able to make the associations easier than others.

- Develop a strategy for dealing with the different levels of learning. Someone with well-formed connections can attach new data to existing networks and learning will take place when you encourage them to connect with what they already know. Someone with less-developed connections will struggle to assimilate new data because of the energy it takes the brain to create new synapses. In this instance breaking learning down into chunks is essential. Use powerful tools such as metaphors, stories and analogies to help people to develop meaningful connections, see patterns develop and make sense of the new data.

- Use the computer analogy to make sense of this. Something with a higher operational specification will function quicker and more effectively than something with a lower specification. That doesn't mean that the lower specification machine (person) is incapable of doing the job, just that you have to spend more time and effort getting it (them) to a stage where it (they) can do it.

I hope that you have been able to follow the thinking behind this model and can see its usefulness in designing coaching sessions. Don't fall into the trap of *thinking* this is only for higher level coaching: the basic principles apply to all levels.

QUESTIONS TO ASK YOURSELF

- How well have I analysed the way my client makes links between issues?
- Have I got a well-developed coaching strategy for dealing with this?

THEORY 24 LEON FESTINGER: COGNITIVE DISSONANCE

Use this when you want to understand why it's difficult to change someone with strong convictions.

Festinger suggested that people continually seek to bring order or meaning to their learning by developing routines and opinions that may give rise to irrational and sometimes maladaptive behaviour. When these routines are disrupted or opinions are contradicted, the individual starts to feel uncomfortable: a state that Festinger referred to as *cognitive dissonance*. This can be depicted as:

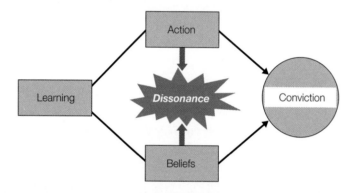

FESTINGER'S THEORY IS BASED ON THREE FUNDAMENTAL ASSUMPTIONS:

People are sensitive to inconsistencies between action and belief.

Recognition of these inconsistencies will cause dissonance which the individual will be motivated to resolve.

Dissonance can be resolved by either: changing their beliefs, changing their actions or changing their perception of action.

Festinger argued that cognitive dissonance makes someone with strong convictions unlikely to change their opinion even if they are presented with a rational argument to the contrary.

HOW TO USE IT

Festinger was inspired to study people's unshakeable conviction in their beliefs when he read an article about a cult whose members believed the earth was going to be destroyed by floods. When the designated apocalypse didn't materialise, committed members, who had given up their homes and jobs, convinced themselves that it was due to their dedication that the world was spared.

You are unlikely to be faced with having to coach too many individuals whose beliefs are that radical, but you need to be wary that there will be some whose convictions are so strong that they will be resistant to your ideas. If you attempt to get them to act in a way that is inconsistent with their convictions, the likelihood is that your efforts will cause cognitive dissonance. Here are two tips to help you deal with this situation:

- Forcing someone to change their beliefs may not be practical so get them to evaluate the actions that arise out of these beliefs. This is one way of getting them to modify their behaviour. You need to be aware however that adverse conditioning (e.g. making them feel bad or guilty about their actions) is not a great way of working with someone and again can have a negative impact and cause even greater cognitive dissonance.

- Try to get an individual to think about their actions in a different manner or context so that they no longer appear to be inconsistent with their beliefs. A good example of this is if you tell someone of a sensitive disposition that their role as a traffic warden is to punish illegal parking, they may experience some dissonance when giving a fine to someone (especially if the person has a disability). Explain that their role is to make sure that all vehicles, including emergency vehicles, will not be deprived access to possible accidents by illegal parking. Do this and dissonance is less likely.

It's important to note that you should never try to get individuals to learn by questioning their unshakable belief on a subject, even if you consider that belief to be inappropriate.

QUESTIONS TO ASK YOURSELF

- Have I appreciated the extent to which the person I am coaching has strong convictions on an issue?
- How certain am I that these convictions need changing?
- How good is my strategy for helping them to change these convictions?

THEORY 25 # MICHAEL MERZENICH: NEUROPLASTICITY

Use this when you want a much deeper understanding of what may be preventing someone from achieving their desired state.

Neuroplasticity is described by Merzenich as the property that the brain possesses that allows it to change its function and its structure through its perception of the world, life experiences and imagination. According to Merzenich, there are generally two types of neuroplasticity:

- **Functional**: Related to the brain's ability to transfer functions from a damaged area of the brain to an undamaged area.
- **Structural**: Related to the brain's ability to change its physical make up as a result of learning.

Merzenich suggests that there are four principles that underpin neuroplasticity.

THESE ARE:

Age variability: Although plasticity is a lifetime occurrence, some types of changes are more predominant at certain stages in someone's life.

Process variety: Although plasticity is an ongoing process, it involves brain cells other than neurons, such as optical and vascular cells.

Reasons: It can happen as a result of damage to the brain, learning or memory formation.

Nature and nurture: Although the environment plays an important role in the process, genetics can also have an influence.

This theory is based on the premise that intelligence is not fixed or planted firmly in our brains from birth but is something that forms and adapts throughout our lives. Despite the fact that the concept of *neuroplasticity* is broad, vague and hardly new, many writers, including Merzenich, claim that it is one of the most important discoveries about the brain.

HOW TO USE IT

Adam suffered with a type of autism. He was a pupil at the special school where my wife worked. He had very limited social skills and communication ability. What he did have was exceptional IT skills. If anything went wrong with any of the PCs, he was the one the staff turned to for help. Computers were his life; he spent most of his time at school and home working on them. The downside of this was that, when he did talk, his speech was in Americanised computer-speak. There are ethical considerations about whether Adam's transfer of functions from one part of his brain (the damaged parts that caused his autism) to the undamaged parts (the parts that contain the logic and reasoning that underpin his talent in IT) should have been discouraged and his social and communication skills encouraged.

I don't have the answer to this dilemma. Neglecting Adam's social development was wrong, but taking Adam away from his computer would have been like chopping his right arm off. Here are some tips for how to apply the theory when coaching people who may be facing barriers affecting their development:

- Start by creating a relaxed state by providing an atmosphere that has the right balance of significant challenge and understanding of the person's feelings and attitudes. Don't make the challenge too difficult or threatening or else you run the risk of damaging someone's confidence or self-esteem.
- Immerse the individual in the subject matter at hand by use of different approaches and by making it relevant to their needs. Discuss the issue in such a way as to allow the individual to develop their own meaningful patterns of interpretation of the subject matter.
- Allow the individual to take charge of the process in a way that is meaningful to them, but support this process by asking challenging questions and encouraging reflection. Encouraging the processing of information in this way will help someone to recognise and deal with their own biases and attitudes.

Creating the ideal environment where the brain is allowed to function at its full potential isn't always possible. Your challenge as a coach is to find the conditions that are ideal for the people who you are coaching. A good starting point may be to reflect on the learning environments where you flourished.

QUESTIONS TO ASK YOURSELF

- Am I creating the right levels of variety, challenge and use of imagination in my coaching?
- Have I created the right environment where talent will flourish?

SECTION 9

DEALING WITH CHALLENGING BEHAVIOUR

INTRODUCTION

Challenging behaviour is not just about people acting in an abusive or disruptive manner during a coaching session, it also includes people who choose not to engage when you are coaching them. Many of the coaching models in the next part of this book are predicated on the belief that the person you are coaching actually wants to be coached. Unfortunately this may not always be the case and you will have to deal with this.

People who choose not to respond positively to coaching do so because they either fail to recognise that they have a problem or refuse to accept that they need to change. Looking at some of the motivational techniques in Theories 5–7 may help here. If the problem you are facing as a coach goes deeper, you may have to look at the theories in this section to help you to resolve these.

I've chosen three theories that I believe offer an interesting perspective on behaviour modification. I think that reading Theories 5–7 alongside the theories in this section will equip you to deal with almost any situation where you are faced with having to coach people with challenging behaviour.

THEORY 26 KURT LEWIN: RESHAPING BEHAVIOUR

Use this when you want to help someone to change their behaviour.

Lewin suggested that learning was linked with changing behaviour and devised a three-stage model for moulding behaviour in which he drew the analogy with changing the shape of an ice cube by unfreezing the old shape, moulding the desired shape and refreezing the new shape.

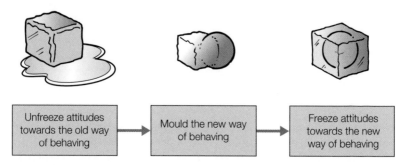

| Unfreeze attitudes towards the old way of behaving | → | Mould the new way of behaving | → | Freeze attitudes towards the new way of behaving |

If you are working with someone who needs to change their behaviour, there are key actions in each of the three stages which you can try.

THESE ARE:

Unfreezing: To get them to understand why the change must take place and to challenge underlying assumptions about themselves and their relationship with others.

Change: To deal with the uncertainty created in the unfreezing stage by helping them to understand how the change in behaviour will benefit them and supporting them to learn how to do things in a different way.

Refreezing: To encourage them to embrace the new ways of doing things by making sure that they incorporate the changes into all of the things that they do.

Lewin argues that by looking at changing behaviour as a process with distinct stages you won't blunder blindly into trying to change someone and will prepare them for the transition.

HOW TO USE IT

Lewin once wrote that there is 'nothing so practical than a good theory'. In Lewin's case many good theories. If there was a *Hall of Fame* for learning theorists, he would be one of the *Victor Ludorum* winners. If we accept the basic premise that learning hasn't happened until change of behaviour has taken place, then this model and Lewin's *Force Field Analysis* are two models that have great application to practice. Here are some steps that you may wish to consider for coaching someone who needs to make personal changes:

- Be absolutely clear that they know what changes they want to make and why they are necessary. Before you start the process of unfreezing, advise them to be prepared to challenge the beliefs, values and behaviours that may be barriers to change.
- Get them to accept that the unfreezing stage is the most complex of the stages as they may be naturally reluctant to accept changes to their established mind set and routines. Try to overcome this reluctance by telling them that the change is necessary and will make them a better person.
- When they are ready to change their behaviour get them to go with their instincts, study role models (see Theory 22) to see how they behave and use positive self-talk to start to embrace the changes (see Theory 16).
- After they have remodelled their behaviour, get them to test out the new behaviours through trial and error (see Theory 21). This will either reinforce the changes or create a new learning cycle. If the tests are positive get them to start to embed the new behaviours into the person they are becoming.

QUESTIONS TO ASK YOURSELF

- Have I determined why someone may be reluctant to change behaviour?
- What must I do to get someone to come out of their comfort zone?

THEORY 27   # PETER HONEY: BEHAVIOUR MODIFICATION

Use this when you want to help people to identify what causes their undesired behaviour and how to deal with this.

Honey suggests that if we need to support someone to change their behaviour, we need to work with them to identify what's causing their present behaviour. Honey argues that internal aspects such as feelings, values and emotions are very often the main cause of bad behaviour and that looking for the signs that trigger the behaviour is the first stage in a three-phase model that can be represented as follows:

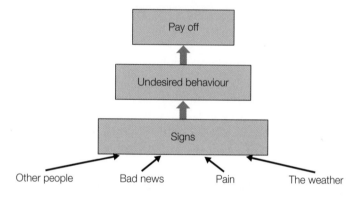

THE KEY ACTIONS IN EACH OF THE THREE PHASES ARE:

Signs: This is the incident that sets off the behaviour. It could be a word or an action.

Behaviour: This is what happens as a reaction to the incident. It could be an act of aggression or withdrawal.

Pay-off: This is the consequence of the behaviour.

Honey claims that we need to tackle both the signs that are the basis for the cause of the undesired behaviour and the pay-off in order to achieve long-term change in behaviour.

HOW TO USE IT

When you are faced with coaching a person whose behaviour is a cause for concern, it may be that, in the past, their behaviour has been ignored or dealt with through some form of external training or disciplinary action. Although some of these actions may have had some success, if the behaviour is still an issue, any successes would have been short-term. Here's a true story to illustrate this:

> Moussa is ten and has severe behavioural issues. Normally he will sit in class doing his work with minimal fuss and attention. When one of his classmates, Sadiq, enters the room, Moussa goes into an uncontrollable frenzy, shouting and waving his arms. There doesn't appear to be any history of antagonism between Moussa and Sadiq, and Sadiq is a mild individual who does nothing to provoke Moussa. The only redress that Moussa's teachers have is to remove him from the class to what they call the Zone. This is a quiet area away from the main classroom where pupils are encouraged to reflect on their action. After about an hour of reflection, Moussa usually returns to the classroom as if nothing has happened. At his appraisal, with teachers and parents, Moussa's mother asked if he could be allowed more time in the Zone as he preferred this to being in class.

To make use of Honey's model:

- Start by assessing the extent of the undesired behaviour.
- Decide what impact this is having on others. Look for the signs that may be triggering the undesired behaviour. Focus on signs not causes.
- Determine what the desired behaviour is going to be like and focus on the pay-off of the desired behaviour. Make sure that the pay-off is going to be a deterrent rather than an encouragement for undesired behaviour.
- Have a plan for changing the signs or the pay-offs.

You might feel that this is a very mechanical approach to dealing with what may be deep-rooted values or beliefs. Although it is a structured approach, it is also realistic and simple in its application. Moussa's teachers had spent so much time trying to rationalise why he reacted so badly to Sadiq that they missed the now obvious point that it was the pay-off that caused the undesired behaviour not the signs. Once they stopped taking Moussa to the *Zone* he realised the pay-off was not what he wanted and he no longer reacted so badly to Sadiq.

QUESTIONS TO ASK YOURSELF

- Does the person I am coaching fully understand the impact of their undesired behaviour?
- Have I identified what's triggering this behaviour?
- Will the pay-off have the impact we need it to have?

THEORY 28 ROBERT HARE: PSYCHOPATHIC CHECKLIST

Use this to understand the behaviour of some of the more challenging people that you will encounter.

Hare developed the Psychopathic Checklist (PCL) as a means of diagnosing psychopathic traits in individuals for clinical, legal or research purposes. Here is a summary of how I have adapted Hare's theory, using my own headings, to show how the key traits could be found in the people who you are coaching.

KEY PSYCHOPATHIC TRAITS:

The Seducer: Charming you and others in a glib and superficial manner and trying to be in charge of the coaching session.

The Ego-maniac: Having an exaggeratedly high estimation of their ability and refusing to accept criticism.

The Sponge: Constantly needing to be stimulated and disrupting coaching sessions that they felt were not challenging enough.

The Procrastinator: Always coming up with excuses for not meeting set objectives.

The Shell: Showing no remorse or guilt if they offend you or others through inappropriate comments.

The Unmovable: Displaying callousness and a lack of empathy with others who may not share their points of view.

The Parasite: Living off the knowledge and skills of their colleagues and falsely claiming credit for ideas.

The Deflector: Failing to accept responsibility for their own actions and seeking to blame others.

The Results Merchant: Lacking any drive for long-term development and being obsessed with passing assignments.

The Disrupter: Displaying a tendency to act impulsively and irresponsibly and causing disharmony among others they may be working with.

The Delinquent: Having poor control over their behaviour and annoying or upsetting their peers.

The actual PCL test is administered by trained professionals and done under strict clinical conditions. The model is only used here for illustrative purposes and serves to highlight extremes in people's behaviours that you may encounter.

HOW TO USE IT

Jon Ronson's interpretation of Hare's theory in *The Psychopath Test* (Picador, 2012) is a humorous account of his encounters with people displaying some of the traits indicated by Hare. Should you have to coach people displaying these traits in your organisation, I would advise you to keep the following in mind:

- Start by assuming that they will always do the worst thing possible within their trait characteristic.

- Have a strategy in mind for handling the worst possible scenario. If they don't do the worst thing possible, celebrate with a quiet drink and save the strategy for next time. If they do the worst possible thing, keep a clear head and follow the old boxing maxim of defending yourself at all times.

- Implement the planned strategy and keep a record of everything that was said or done. You can still have a quiet drink, but this time to relax.

- Whatever course of action you take, make sure that you follow the rules and regulations set down by your organisation for dealing with people. Even if you were in the right, failure to adhere to correct procedures could result in legal action against you or your organisation.

It's worth making the point here that you will also almost certainly display some of these traits. You need to reflect on this and explore the impact that you have on others.

QUESTIONS TO ASK YOURSELF

- Am I aware of my own psychopathic traits?
- What's making me think the person I am coaching has psychopathic traits?
- Have I got a strategy in place for dealing with this?

SUMMARY OF PART 1

In Part 1, I have tried to demonstrate the many different ways in which people of all ages, levels and outlooks think and what motivates them to want to learn. I have looked at the relationships between learning and individual growth, learning and personality types, and learning and learning style preferences. The individual learning theories in this part of the book have a significant impact on coaching practice. Each has its particular focus:

- *Behaviourism* is underpinned by conditioning and reinforcement.
- Mental acts are the primary aim of *cognitivism*.
- Experience and self-efficacy are the basis for *humanism*.
- Information processing and memory are the focus of *neurolism.*

Each theory reflects different degrees of human activeness in learning: behaviourist theory relates to *reactive* learning; cognitivist theory relates to *responsive* learning; humanist theory is about *reflective* learning; while neurolism emphasises the importance of *receptive* learning.

The key points to emerge from this part of the book are:

- People learn best when they relate the learning to their own learning goals, knowledge or experiences.
- People have a preference for the way they learn and respond best either by observing, listening or doing.
- Individuals have their own unique approach to thinking and learning.
- Perception and personality will influence the way that people think and learn.
- Although people may have a learning style preference they won't learn just by adhering to this preference.
- Competence is a good baseline for learning but creativity adds value.
- Nobody is perfect.
- If you fail at something try again but this time fail better and keep failing till you get the right result.
- Using an individual's prior experiences can be a very powerful coaching tool.
- An individual will learn best when they feel connected to the subject.
- People should never be afraid of trying out something new.

- If you are supporting someone, consider their feelings and beliefs, avoid being judgemental and don't try to force your values and beliefs on someone.
- Someone with deep convictions on an issue will be a hard person to change.
- Not every person you are coaching wants to be coached.

The most important point to emerge from this is that there is a multitude of personality types and learning styles that make it impossible to draw out a single blueprint that fits all.

PART 2

TAKING IT FURTHER

INTRODUCTION

I n the entries in this part of the book, I have chosen 27 of the most widely used and respected coaching models from which you can choose any one, or any number in combination, to suit whatever coaching situation you are involved in. Although some, such as mindfulness and NLP, may require more reading around the subject to become fully conversant with them, you will find that there is sufficient in all of the entries to go out and apply them.

While the theories used in Part 1 are based on rigour and research, the models included in Part 2 are more speculative, but nevertheless appear to work. The literature on the subject is littered with examples of individuals and organisations that have benefitted from techniques such as GROW or CLEAR, and praise for concepts such as mindfulness or NLP is far-reaching. I've also chosen ideas and models from people such as Gallwey (Theory 38) and Whitmore (Theory 55) who have made significant contributions to the development of coaching as a management tool. Use this part of the book therefore as a toolbox in which *every tool has a purpose and every purpose has a tool*.

The models are presented in alphabetical order, listed by their creators, so as not to convey the impression that any one model is better than another. In this respect all of the models can be used when coaching an individual, team or organisation. I suggest that you go through the toolbox, identify which of the tools may be appropriate and select the one(s) that you want to adapt and adopt to best suit your style of working, the person you are coaching and the context in which the coaching is taking place.

Although I am confident that there is enough information in each of the entries to enable you to apply the model, at the end of the book there is a recommended reading list where you can find out more about each of the models.

RICHARD BANDLER AND JOHN GRINDER: NEURO-LINGUISTIC PROGRAMMING (NLP)

Use this when you want a model for understanding how people habitually think and behave.

The concept of NLP was developed in the early 1970s by Bandler and Grinder. The breakdown of the term defines what NLP is all about:

- **Neuro**: This is how you use your senses to make sense of what's happening, which in turn influences how you feel and what you say and do.
- **Linguistic**: This is the language and communication systems that you use to influence yourself and others.
- **Programming**: This is a succession of steps designed to achieve a particular outcome.

Bandler and Grinder studied the work of a number of therapists who were achieving excellent results with their clients, and modelled some of their techniques which they then presented under what is known as the *Four Pillars of NLP*.

THESE ARE:

Setting your goal: Knowing what you want in any situation.

Using your senses: Paying close attention to the world around you.

Behaving flexibly: Keep on changing what you do until you get what you want.

Building relationships: Being aware of the contribution that others make to helping you achieve your goal.

Bandler and Grinder stress the importance of debunking some of the myths surrounding NLP. They emphasise that it's not a cult nor a process for bending minds but a collection of tools that managers, coaches, mentors, counsellors, in fact anyone involved in any relationship, can use to have a positive influence on the person who they are relating to.

HOW TO USE IT

Here are some important principles to keep in mind, should you choose to use NLP as a coaching tool:

- **The map is not the territory**: Accept that, if the territory represents reality, the map is merely the representation of that reality by the person you are coaching.

- **Respect the other person's map**: Acknowledge that everyone responds according to their individual maps and may act in ways that you find unhelpful or unacceptable.

- **The meaning and outcome of the communication is the response that you get**: Instead of blaming the person you are coaching for misunderstanding your meaning, accept total responsibility for your communication.

- **Every behaviour has a positive intention**: Appreciate that behaviour is created specifically with regard to the context and the reality currently being experienced. Change is necessary when the context and reality changes.

- **Accept the person; change the behaviour**: Understand that the behaviour of the person you are coaching is not who they are. Accept the person but support them to change their behaviour.

- **There is no failure, only feedback**: Reassure the person you are coaching that if they haven't succeeded in something, they haven't failed, they just haven't succeeded yet. Support them to vary their behaviour and find different ways of achieving their desired outcomes.

- **If you always do what you've always done, you'll always get what you've always got**: This is sometimes referred to as Ashby's *Law of Requisite Variety*. Recognise that the individual with the greatest flexibility of thought and behaviour is more likely to control the outcome of any interaction.

If you don't like the overall concept of NLP then check out whether you can use any of the tools and techniques.

QUESTIONS TO ASK YOURSELF

- How is my sense of reality different to that of the person I am coaching?
- Am I sure that the person I am coaching fully understands what I want them to do?
- Do I make sure that the person I am coaching learns from any failures they experience?

GREGORY BATESON: NEURO-LOGICAL LEVELS

Use this when you want to help someone to understand how their behaviours, capabilities, beliefs and values affect how they understand and tackle issues.

Bateson argued that the *neuro-logical levels* model (sometimes just referred to as the *logical levels* model) offered people the opportunity to gain a fresh perspective on what gets in the way of effective change. The model is made up of a number of levels or categories and a hierarchy that indicates the relationship between the categories. The model is usually represented as:

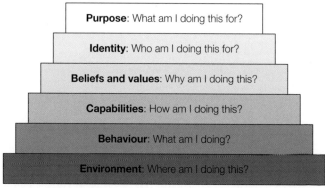

Purpose: What am I doing this for?

Identity: Who am I doing this for?

Beliefs and values: Why am I doing this?

Capabilities: How am I doing this?

Behaviour: What am I doing?

Environment: Where am I doing this?

Source: Dilts, R. (1990) *Changing Belief Systems with Neuro-Linguistic Programming [NLP]*. Capitola, CA: Meta Publications.

EACH CATEGORY IN THE MODEL CAN BE SUMMARISED AS:

Environment: This is the physical environment that we are in. This also includes the people that are around us and the resources that we have at our disposal.

Behaviour: This refers to what we think, say and do and the impact that this has on others.

Capabilities: These are the abilities and skills that we have.

Beliefs and values: These are the things that are important to us and influence our actions.

Identity: This is our own personal sense of self; it defines who we are and what role we fulfil.

Purpose: This is about what drives us to be the person we are or the things that we do.

Bateson argues that when organisations or individuals make changes, they are less likely to succeed if they fail to make the right changes at the most appropriate levels.

HOW TO USE IT

Here's how to coach someone to work through the *neuro-logical* levels:

- Make up six cards (about 40–50 cm square) with each of the categories. Place the cards about a metre apart in order of the hierarchy as they appear in the diagram (*environment* to *purpose*). Get the person you are coaching to start to the left of the *environment* card and get them to consider: 'What is my desired state, who will be there with me and what resources do I have?'

- Now ask them to step onto the *environment* card and visualise themselves in the desired state together with everyone and everything that is significant in this time and space. Once they have clarity of vision, get them to step onto the *behaviour* card and describe what impact their thoughts and actions in the desired state are having on the people who share the environment with them. Encourage them to ask themselves if they need to make changes.

- Only when the vision and realisation of what needs to be done is clear should you let them step onto the *capabilities* card and describe the new skills and abilities that they possess in the desired state. Get them to ask themselves what they need to do to make changes. Get them to step onto the *beliefs and values* card and ask themselves whether there are any conflicts between what they are and what they want to be and how they can resolve these conflicts. Ask them to step onto the *identity* card and visualise who they are once the changes have been made.

- Finally, get them to step onto the *purpose* card and ask themselves if they have a clearly defined sense of purpose. If they have, then they have completed the process. If not then get them to work back down the row of cards in reverse order.

QUESTION TO ASK YOURSELF

- How badly does the individual want to change their behaviour?

THEORY 31 DONALD BROADBENT: FILTERING

Use this when you want to understand how people filter out information that is not relevant to them.

Broadbent argued that our personal sense of reality is created through ways in which we interpret our experiences. This suggests that a person's understanding of information may not be as the other person intended it to be. He argued that this is as a result of a filtering process that either *deletes*, *distorts* or *generalises* the information.

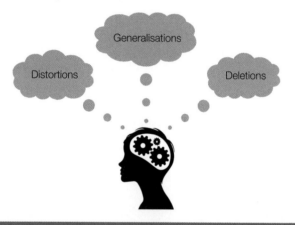

EACH ELEMENT IN THE PROCESS CAN BE SUMMARISED AS:

Deletion: Prevents the person from having to absorb the mass of sensory information that they are exposed to every second and strips the information down to only those bits that are considered relevant.

Distortion: Allows the person to fit information into a framework of pre-existing knowledge.

Generalisation: Enables the person to make a judgement on new information based on something similar they may have experienced previously.

Broadbent maintains that what is actually learnt by individuals is dictated by their own personal filters that in turn are influenced by their *beliefs*, *values* and *memories*. This can often create a state of conflict in the learner's mind as they attempt to reconcile previously held beliefs and values and past experiences with their new knowledge.

HOW TO USE IT

You can never really know exactly how the other person is feeling because you can never really get inside their mind. The same principle applies when you are coaching someone who has interpersonal issues with another person. Here is an example that illustrates this:

> Anna was a trainee teacher who I was coaching. One of the problems she was facing that was making her ill was her reaction to one of her learners. She told me that this girl 'had this look on her face – I just knew she wasn't going to participate in the lesson'. Of course Anna had no idea what the girl was thinking, she was just distorting the information she was receiving from the girl. When I suggested that 'the girl might just have had a bad hair day', Anna laughed and decided to think through a different approach in her next session.

As a coach you need to appreciate that people employ a wealth of filtering systems every time you speak to them. They do this subconsciously to be able to cope with the mass of information (non-verbal as well as verbal) that you are exposing them to. The next time that you have something important to convey to them:

- Make sure that you think through beforehand what outcome you expect as a result of conveying the message. Be specific in determining this. Start with the expression 'by the end of the session you will be able to…' or better still ask them what do they expect to be able to achieve by the end of the session?
- Make sure that you appreciate what filters the person you are coaching may be using and how these might affect how they interpret your message. Look at and listen attentively to their responses.
- Try to interpret from the verbal and non-verbal clues if they are responding in the way you want them to, but never make assumptions about what they are thinking. If the clues are not clear then ask them directly: 'What are you thinking?'

Above all else, don't be afraid to try a different approach if what you are doing isn't working.

QUESTIONS TO ASK YOURSELF

- How certain am I that the person I am coaching is interpreting what I want them to do correctly?
- How can I avoid making assumptions about this?

THEORY 32   MARTY BROUNSTEIN: THE FIVE PILLARS FOR BUILDING COMMITMENT

Use this when you want a model for building commitment to performance improvement.

Brounstein suggests that having a high level of commitment from the people that you are coaching will result in high levels of performance and a greater level of staff retention. He argues that coaching is one of the best ways of inspiring employee commitment and offers his *Five Pillars for Building Commitment* as a model for achieving this. The pillars can be represented as:

THE FIVE PILLARS CAN BE SUMMARISED AS:

Focus: When the focus pillar is strong, the person you are coaching will know what's expected of them, the direction in which the organisation is going and what its priorities are.

Involvement: When the involvement pillar is strong, the person you are coaching will feel a sense of inclusion and empowerment and is more likely to contribute towards planning, problem-solving and decision-making.

Development: When the development pillar is strong, the person you are coaching will feel encouraged to take advantage of opportunities for learning and personal growth.

Gratitude: When the gratitude pillar is strong, the person you are coaching will feel that their contribution has been valued.

Accountability: When the accountability pillar is strong, the person you are coaching will accept more responsibility in the job, confident that they have the authority to see it through.

The philosophy underpinning Brounstein's model is that, while good coaches focus on performance, they must also recognise that people are connected to the work that they do. In this respect, Brounstein advocates that laying the foundations for building commitment requires focusing on developing working relationships as well as developing the performance of the individual.

HOW TO USE IT

Here are some steps to help you lay strong foundation blocks:

- Ensure the person you are coaching knows what's expected of them. Start by setting goals and agreeing performance plans. Define the results expected from a task and the parameters that they have to work within on the task. Discuss and agree priorities and clarify needs and expectations.

- Show them that they have a say in the factors that affect their work. Make sure that you agree performance targets and allow employees to determine how best to achieve these targets. Try to get their involvement by encouraging them to take the lead in coaching sessions.

- Encourage and support individuals who want to take up developmental opportunities. Discuss what learning they need to be more effective and develop an action plan for addressing these needs. Make sure that you set plans with individuals for reinforcing any professional development undertaken.

- Recognise and acknowledge contributions by giving regular feedback when a task is being undertaken and making a note of appreciating efforts as well as results.

- Ensure that responsibility is given and high standards are upheld by conducting regular performance review meetings. Make sure that you give positive feedback when performance is up to standard and negative feedback when it slips. Allow the person you are coaching the opportunity to rectify any mistakes they have made.

QUESTIONS TO ASK YOURSELF

- How can I make sure that I have developed a good working relationship with the person I am coaching?
- Do we both know what's expected of each other?

THEORY 33 ARTHUR COSTA AND BENA KALLICK: THE COACH AS A CRITICAL FRIEND

Use this when you want to challenge or critique someone with good intent.

Costa and Kellick describe a *critical friend* as a trusted person who asks provocative questions, provides a different perspective on an issue facing someone and critiques their actions with good intent. They outline a process for the critical friend/individual interaction that can be depicted as:

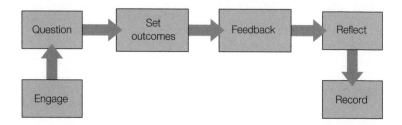

THE ELEMENTS IN THE PROCESS CAN BE SUMMARISED AS:

Engagement: The individual outlines the problem and asks the critical friend for feedback.

Questioning: The critical friend asks questions in order to understand the root causes of the problem and to clarify the context in which the problem is occurring.

Desired outcomes: The individual sets the desired outcomes for the interaction, thus ensuring they are in control.

Feedback: The critical friend provides feedback on what seems to be significant about the problem. This feedback should be more than a cursory look at the problem and should provide an alternative viewpoint that helps address the problem.

Reflection: Both parties reflect on what was discussed.

Recording: The individual records their views on the points and suggestions raised. The critical friend records the advice given and makes a note of what follow-up action they need to take.

Costa and Kellick argue that the coach as a critical friend is a very powerful idea, perhaps because it contains an inherent tension within the term: friends bring a high degree of unconditional positive regard, whereas critics may be negative and intolerant of failure. They describe the ideal as a marriage of unconditional support and unconditional critique.

HOW TO USE IT

Here are some tips to help you become a good critical friend:

- Don't allow your friendship with the client to obscure the real issue that they are faced with. Too much stress on the friendship side of the role may compromise the need for a deep and critical exchange of views. Sympathising with their plight will get you nowhere and may even have a detrimental effect on coming up with a solution. The aim is to stimulate divergent thinking by introducing different views and fresh insights.

- Have a clear understanding of the boundaries that exist in the relationship and set clear objectives of who will do what and by when. Make sure that you review progress on the objectives at regular intervals. Provide honest and critical feedback to your client and be willing to accept honest and critical feedback from your client. Finally, reflect on the nature and appropriateness of the relationship and ask whether this needs revising.

QUESTIONS TO ASK YOURSELF

- How certain am I that there is a clear distinction between my role as coach and that of friend?
- Are the boundaries clear to both of us?
- Am I giving feedback in an honest and critical manner?

THEORY 34 EDWARD DE BONO: THE SIX THINKING HATS

Use this when you want your people to be more creative in the way they deal with problems.

De Bono argues that in order for someone to be more creative in the way that they approach problems, they have to get a more rounded view of a situation and have to move outside of their habitual thinking modes. He developed his *thinking hats* technique as a means of encouraging people to be more rounded and creative in the way they approached solving problems. In this technique, you simply wear the hat (actually or figuratively) depending on which approach you need to adopt.

THE CHARACTERISTICS OF THE SIX HATS WHEN COACHING SOMEONE ARE:

White hat: Focus on the information available; get them to see what they can learn from this.

Red hat: Rely on intuition and emotion; get them to try to understand the responses they get.

Black hat: Look at the negative points; get them to try to see the weaknesses in an idea.

Yellow hat: Look at the positive points; get them to try to see the strengths in an idea.

Green hat: Develop creative solutions; encourage them not to be afraid to make suggestions no matter how off-the-wall they seem.

Blue hat: Take control of the situation; show them how this helps them to get things going when they start to stall.

De Bono suggests that creative thinking is the most basic human skill and one on which both social and economic progress depends. He also argues that it is the area that most individuals and organisations neglect.

HOW TO USE IT

Look at this example for some tips on how to use *thinking hats* as a coaching tool:

Let's assume that you have been asked to coach a manager who wants to become a coach. Most of the models in this part of the book advocate undertaking some form of analysis of why the person wants to be coached and what they expect from the coaching. After you've explained the *thinking hats* process to them, they grab the *black hat* and start telling you all the reasons why they don't think they'll make a good coach. Here's what to do next:

- After listening attentively, you ask them to put on the *white hat* and start to look at the facts. Find out if they know how much it costs the organisation to train people and how much they could save by coaching. Get them to clarify what other benefits being a good coach will have for the individuals in the organisation.

- Once a good case for coaching has been established get them to put on the *red hat* and explore what it will mean to them personally to be recognised as a good coach. Ask how they are feeling now. Don't be alarmed if they reach for the *black hat*, as identifying and addressing issues early on in the process is a good thing. You may have to go through *white* and *red* hats again before they begin to feel more optimistic about being a coach and start wearing the *yellow hat*.

- As their optimism increases, encourage them to put the *green hat* on and to start visualising how they will operate as a coach. This is the creative stage of the process that will require them to look at things in new ways.

- You may think this is the end of the process, but what about that *blue hat* lurking at the bottom of the pile. This is the control hat. Most of the really good coaching models make the point that coaching is a two-way process that involves feedback and reflection. Give the person you are coaching the opportunity to tell you what they think about your coaching and ways you could improve: a case of coachee turned coach.

QUESTIONS TO ASK YOURSELF

- Have I done the pre-coaching analysis and listened attentively to their responses?

- Have I got them to think creatively?

- Have I made sure that I have sought feedback and am prepared to act on this?

THEORY 35 # ROBERT DILTS: THE DISNEY CREATIVITY STRATEGY

Use this when you want to support someone to be more creative in their thinking.

Dilts claimed that the biggest barrier to people acting creatively is the tendency to shoot down new ideas before they even get off the runway by pointing out all of the reasons why something won't work. Dilts modelled a number of great minds, fictional and real, to find out why they were successful. One of the people who he modelled was Walt Disney. Dilts argued that Disney possessed enormous creativity and inventiveness that in the film world was second to none. Through modelling him, Dilts discovered three facets to his creative strategy; the dreamer, the realist and the critic.

EACH OF THESE FACETS CAN BE SUMMARISED AS FOLLOWS:

Dreamer: This is where you imagine any possibilities that may exist. Allow a random series of thoughts to flow. Don't stop to make judgements no matter how absurd the idea may appear.

Realist: This is the pragmatic part of the process where you look at how to make the ideas work in practice. Now's the time to start considering whether the dream can work in the real world.

Critic: This is the evaluative stage where you judge whether or not the idea will satisfy what you want to achieve. During this stage you may choose to abort the idea or make whatever refinements are necessary for you to reach your goal.

Dilts suggests that the *Disney creative strategy* is a simple but powerful process that can be used with groups, individuals or as a self-development tool.

HOW TO USE IT

Imagine that you are working as a coach with a dysfunctional group of people. The group leader is boring and conservative in his outlook. His partner is looking for more excitement and variation in her work and the two junior members of the team feel they are in a rut and become rebellious. Sounds a bit like the plot to *Mary Poppins*.

Often thought of as Disney's greatest achievement, *Mary Poppins* is the story of a coaching specialist (masquerading as a nanny) who is tasked with changing the behaviour of members of the Banks' group (or family). She uses the *Disney creative strategy* by turning each member of the group into dreamers and taking them into a fantasy world of fairground rides, steeplechasing and penguins. When the group leader comes back into the real world he decides that they have better options and develops a plan of how to make these options work. Mary Poppins' work is completed and she jets off to meet her next client.

I guess that I couldn't resist using a Disney movie plot here. Here is a great process for using this model:

- Set out a room with the three cards (each should be 40–50 cm square and about two metres apart) with headings *Dreamer*, *Realist* and *Critic*. Get the person you are coaching to stand on the *Dreamer* card and in a relaxed state start to visualise their desired state. When they are in this state, get them to ask themselves: 'How will I feel? What will I see or hear?' Get them to step off the *Dreamer* card and into a neutral area (not on any of the three cards) and just collect their thoughts for a few moments.

- The next step is to get them to step onto the *Realist* card and to start thinking about what needs to be done to make the dream a reality. When they are in this state, get them to ask themselves: 'How will I know when I have reached the desired state? What needs to happen? Who needs to be involved? What's the first step I need to take?' Get them to go back into the neutral zone and if necessary make a list of the things that they need to do. Start to agree a plan of action with them.

- The final act is to get them to step onto the *Critic* card and to evaluate the feasibility of the plan. When they are in this state, get them to ask themselves: 'What or who can prevent me from reaching my desired state? What can I do to overcome this? What's missing in the plan?' Get them to go back into the neutral zone and decide if they now have a creative, well thought out plan of action. If they have, then support them to achieve it. If not, get them to go through the loop as many times as necessary to achieve it.

(Just don't keep singing *supercalli*… etc. as they move between the cards!)

QUESTION TO ASK YOURSELF

- How good is the person I am coaching at visualising what their ideal state is?

THEORY 36 GERARD EGAN: THE SKILLED HELPER MODEL

Use this when you want to support someone to manage their own problems.

Egan's *skilled helper model* is a three-stage model in which the objective is to achieve lasting change and empower people to manage their own problems more effectively. The model can be depicted as:

THE THREE STAGES CAN BE SUMMARISED AS:

Exploration: The purpose here is to build a non-threatening relationship with the other person and help them to explore their current situation by identifying and clarifying problems and opportunities and assessing their ability to deal with these.

Challenge: The purpose here is to help support the other person in developing a more in-depth and objective understanding of their situation by encouraging them to question what their real needs and wants are and what other possibilities they could consider.

Action: The purpose here is to help the other person to turn good intentions into actual results by helping them to set specific, measurable, achievable, realistic objectives with a timescale for achieving them.

Egan argues that the *skilled helper* approach encourages people to become active interpreters of the world by giving meaning to actions, events and situations. He also stresses the importance of people facing up to and overcoming challenges and problems and seeking out new opportunities.

HOW TO USE IT

Here are some tips to help you become a skilled helper:

- Find out what is happening to the other person in their words and then reflect it back to them without prejudice or making judgements. Start this process with some open-ended questions and listen attentively to their response and focus on what is being said, not what you plan to say. Make sure that you keep your own views to yourself and focus on the issues that are important to the other person. Ensure that you have fully understood what the issues are by paraphrasing and reflecting back to them. Summarise the key points to emerge from the discussion. Make sure that you have agreement on these.

- If you have been successful in establishing rapport with the other person any reluctance or resistance that may have been present in the exploration stage will have been overcome. Don't be afraid of revisiting stage one if you are still encountering resistance. Take each issue one at a time and encourage the other person to think about whether there are other ways of looking at the issue. Get them to look at the issue through other people's eyes. Encourage them to explore various options and strategies, as well as helping them to understand and overcome the barriers they may be facing. Don't leave this stage without the other person's willingness to identify areas for development. Get them to record these.

- If the other person is now receptive to making changes, it's time to turn good intentions into action, so get them to come up with as many strategies as they can. Help them to focus on those actions that are viable in terms of the existing situation, their needs and aspirations and the resources they have. Some of these actions may involve a series of small steps rather than one massive step. A few early successes will build the individual's confidence to tackle something more substantial and challenging. Don't leave this stage without agreeing a follow-up meeting to establish what progress the other person has made. Avoid being judgemental if they haven't made progress but don't be afraid of questioning their commitment to changing.

Now think about two issues where you had to help someone to handle change. Choose one that had a positive result and one that had a negative result.

QUESTIONS TO ASK YOURSELF

- What did I do that had an impact on whether the result was good or bad?
- Could I have handled it differently?
- Can I apply this new approach to the person I am currently coaching?

THEORY 37 **FERDINAND FOURNIES: COACHING DISCUSSION PLAN**

Use this when you want a plan for face-to-face coaching.

Fournies refers to face-to-face coaching as the *coaching discussion*. He suggests that the purpose of this is to redirect an individual's behaviour towards solving a problem or correcting a performance issue. He proposes a five-step model that follows on from the analysis of what needs to be done. The process can be represented as:

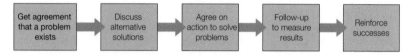

Get agreement that a problem exists → Discuss alternative solutions → Agree on action to solve problems → Follow-up to measure results → Reinforce successes

Fournies argues that the coaching discussion will not work unless obstacles identified in the coaching analysis have been removed. He also advocates that, if obstacles occur during the discussion, the conversation should be terminated and the coach should revert back to analysing what the cause of the obstacle is and addressing this before returning to the conversation.

HOW TO USE IT

The coaching discussion follows on from some form of coaching analysis in which reasons for finding out why people are not doing what they should be doing are identified. This process will involve answering a number of questions like: Does the individual know their performance is unsatisfactory? Do they know what is supposed to be done? Do they have the resources or skills to do it? Are their obstacles preventing them from doing it? Do they have the right levels of energy and motivation to make it work? Only when you have completed this analysis should you enter into the coaching discussion. If you have reached this stage here are some tips to bear in mind during the conversation:

■ Get agreement that a problem exists. Don't assume that the individual is aware that there is a problem – this is a recipe for disaster. You may find it hard to believe but many problem employees suspect they are doing something wrong but don't accept it as a problem. Get them to recognise it as a problem by pointing out the implications of what they are doing wrong to themselves, their colleagues and the organisation.

- Sit down with the individual and discuss what options are available to address the problem. Remember, it's the behaviour, not the person that you are looking to change. Because of this, specify those aspects of behaviour where changes are necessary in order to influence the outcome of the coaching.

- Work with the individual to gain mutual agreement on which of the options are feasible. A good way of doing this is to look at the strengths and weaknesses of each option and the opportunities and threats that you both will be faced with in pursuing them. Once you have a list of preferred options, decide what action will be necessary and when it should be undertaken.

- Don't waste all the time you have spent in analysing the problem and discussing options by failing to follow-up and checking that the action has been completed successfully. Don't fall into the trap of seeing some early improvements and assuming your job is done. Effective follow-up includes regular feedback and reinforcement of good behaviour.

Never underestimate the impact that reinforcing any achievement has on the individual. People will rarely reach self-actualisation or even self-esteem (see Theory 17) without your recognition of what they have achieved. Do this as soon as possible after the achievement for maximum impact.

QUESTIONS TO ASK YOURSELF

- Have I got recognition from the individual that a problem exists?
- Have we reached agreement on a range of alternatives to address the problem?

THEORY 38 TIM GALLWEY: THE INNER GAME

Use this when you want to understand how people's capacity to perform can be affected by internal as well as external influences.

Gallwey used sporting analogies taken from tennis, skiing and golf to demonstrate how coaching in any capacity can be used to unlock a person's potential to maximise their own performance. His main premise was that it was 'the opponent in one's head' that was more formidable than any external obstacle.

His basic philosophy is summed up in the formula:

Performance = Potential – Interference

In this respect Gallwey argues that, the main task of the coach is to reduce or remove the 'interferences' that block the individual or team from reaching their optimum levels of performance. Gallwey maintains that, in order to achieve this, a coach must engage in three stages of conversation.

THESE CAN BE SUMMARISED AS:

Awareness: The stage where the situation is clearly defined and understood by all parties.

Choice: This is the development of conscious perception which involves broadening the vision of how to get to a desired outcome.

Trust: This is where the coach and the person being coached have unshakable faith in each other's capacity to deliver the goods.

Gallwey was perhaps the first writer to suggest a simple but comprehensive method of coaching that could be applied to almost any coaching situation. His ideas have influenced a number of leading exponents of business coaching. He defines 'really good coaches' as those who make the people being coached believe in themselves, their values and their capabilities.

HOW TO USE IT

Gallwey was something of an enigma. Not only was he a respected tennis coach but also a Harvard educationalist. When he first applied his theories of tennis coaching to management, few coaches embraced his ideas. His books however were very popular with sports professionals. What he did do was to challenge the belief that coaches should be autocratic bullies and the behaviourist view that people are little more than empty vessels that need to be filled. He did this by applying the principles of *awareness*, *choice* and *trust*. Here are some tips for how to do this:

- The **awareness** stage is simply the step of defining the situation clearly. Don't impose your perception of the situation and don't tell the individual what you are going to do. Use this stage as a way of building up rapport with the individual by asking them what their perception of the situation is. Ask them what they want out of the coaching and what coaching methods they feel comfortable with. Draw up a set of objectives that are specific, measurable, achievable and timebound.

- The **choice** stage is about examining the options available that will achieve the desired objectives. Do some form of board blasting activity where all options are written down regardless of how unrealistic they may appear; it's the process of getting a list that's important. Now do the reality check and discount the options that are not feasible. Prioritise the ones that are left. You may wish to do this separately and then compare notes. Discuss which option(s) will work best and agree an action plan.

- By now, because everything to date has been done with, not to the individual, they should begin to feel respected, valued and able to move forward with **trust** and confidence. The best coaches are those who make the person they are coaching believe in themselves, feel valued and trust in their own abilities. This can only be achieved if the individual trusts in the coach's ability and intentions.

Achieving this level of coaching won't be easy. You need a mindset that acts as a framework for everything that you do. This includes a good understanding of how people learn (see Theories 1–4), your methods of communication (see Theories 8–10), your motivational techniques (see Theories 5–7) and your value structure. Don't be fazed by this, these are attributes that you can learn!

QUESTIONS TO ASK YOURSELF

- Have we defined the situation clearly?
- Have we fully explored the options available to achieve the desired outcomes?
- Does the individual trust me?

THEORY 39   HOWARD GARDNER: MULTIPLE INTELLIGENCE

Use this when you want to understand how people process information in a way that is unique to them.

Gardner proposed that human beings have several types of intelligence that formed the potential to process information in a range of different contexts and cultures.

GARDNER'S ORIGINAL SEVEN INTELLIGENCES WERE:

Linguistic: The capacity to understand and use spoken and written language.

Logical-Mathematical: The capacity to analyse problems logically.

Bodily-Kinaesthetic: The capacity to use and interpret expressive movement.

Visual-Spatial: The capacity to recognise patterns and dimensions.

Musical: The capacity to compose, perform and appreciate musical patterns.

Interpersonal: The capacity to understand the intentions, motivations and desires of others.

Intrapersonal: The capacity to understand one's own feelings, fears and needs.

HE LATER ADDED THREE MORE INTELLIGENCES:

Naturalistic: The capacity to recognise and categorise objects in nature.

Spiritual: The capacity to rationalise thoughts around human existence.

Existential: The capacity to tackle deep questions about the meaning of life.

Gardner made two fundamental claims about his ideas: firstly, that they accounted for the full range of human cognition and, secondly, that each individual had a unique blend of the various intelligences that made them into who they are.

HOW TO USE IT

Identifying individual differences among a group of individuals will help you to be better at understanding the learning process and more prepared to work with people. You will appreciate from Gardner's theories that people possess a range of intelligences and process information differently. Let's look at this in the context of a challenge:

Imagine that you are appearing as a cookery coach on one of those television celebrity cooking contests. Your guests in the great bake-off are: J.K. Rowling (author of the *Harry Potter* books), Stephen Hawking (theoretical physicist), Darcey Bussell (prima ballerina), Vivienne Westwood (fashion guru), Adele Adkins (Oscar-winning singer songwriter), Air Vice-Marshall Elaine West (the UK's most senior female military officer), Richard Branson (entrepreneur), Alan Titchmarsh (television presenter), Angela Berners-Wilson (the UK's first woman to be ordained as a Church of England Priest) and Douglas Adams (creator of *The Hitchhiker's Guide to the Galaxy*). Your role is to teach your guests how to prepare your speciality dish. Look at the following table and fill in the end column.

Guest	Main intelligence	How would you teach them to cook?
J.K. Rowling	Manipulating words and playing with language	
Stephen Hawking	Working on logical problems and complex operations	
Darcey Bussell	Participating in activities involving movement and touch	
Vivienne Westwood	Experimenting with shapes and colours	
Adele	Listening to music and composing songs	
AVM Elaine West	Working in groups and directing them	
Richard Branson	Working independently on challenging tasks	
Alan Titchmarsh	Working with natural products	
The Rev Angela Berners-Wilson	Meditating and reflecting on important issues	
Douglas Adams	Searching for a deeper meaning of life	

Now that you have shown them how to cook, look at how you could apply these principles to your own coaching.

QUESTIONS TO ASK YOURSELF

- Am I aware of how the person I am coaching processes information?
- Have I planned my coaching sessions to take account of this?

THEORY 40 ANDREW GILBERT AND KAREN WHITTLEWORTH: THE OSCAR MODEL

Use this when you want to have a solution-focused coaching model.

Gilbert and Whittleworth suggest that solution-focused coaching differs from other approaches in that it focuses on solutions rather than problems. They claim that their model is designed to discover what is working well and to replicate that, rather than continuing to do what is not working well. The model is based on the OSCAR acronym and can be depicted as:

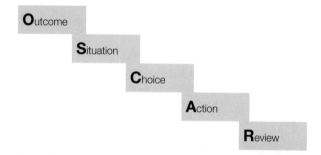

Outcome
Situation
Choice
Action
Review

THE CONSTITUENTS OF THE MODEL CAN BE SUMMARISED AS:

Outcome: This is where the coach determines what the individual wants to achieve.

Situation: This is where the coach clarifies what the individual's current situation is.

Choice: This is where the coach and the individual discuss what options are available and the consequences of making particular choices.

Action: This is where the coach encourages the individual to take responsibility for their own action plan.

Review: This is an opportunity for both the individual and coach to reflect on the interventions so far and evaluate what's worked well and what needs to be modified.

Gilbert and Whittleworth suggest that their model will bring out the existing skills and capabilities of the client and that ownership of the process is transferred from the coach to the client.

Mark McKergow and Paul Jackson offer a slightly different version of the model by replacing *choice* with *know-how and resources* (making OSKAR). This is where the coach uncovers the client's skills, knowledge and attributes and what resources they have available to them.

HOW TO USE IT

The principle of transferring ownership of the coaching process by stimulating the person being coached to analyse their own situation and articulating how they can change is a good way of thinking about the OSCAR/OSKAR models. The essence of good coaching, using this model, is getting the person being coached to visualise where they are, where they want to be and how you, as the coach, can support them to get there. Here are some useful tips and questions that you can ask the person being coached in each stage:

- Determine the desired outcomes by asking: 'What do you want to achieve by working with me? What specifically do you want to achieve from the present session? How will you know when you have achieved the outcome?'

- Clarify where the client is currently by asking: 'Where do you see yourself now? What specifically has happened for you to get there? What do you consider to be your strengths and weaknesses?'

- Discuss what options are available by asking: 'What are the opportunities and threats facing you? What specifically are the consequences to you of these? What will happen if you don't face up to them?'

- Decide what needs to be done next by asking: 'What is going well? What specifically is the next step to take? How will you know when you have achieved this step?'

- Confirm that the client is on the right course by asking: 'What did you do to make the changes happen? What specifically are the effects that the changes have had? What do you think will change next?'

If you prefer the OSKAR model, simply replace *choices* with *know-how* and determine what resources are available by asking: What helps you to perform at the level you are at now? What specifically are the skills, knowledge and attributes you have? What will happen if you don't improve your know-how?

QUESTIONS TO ASK YOURSELF

- Have I pinned them down by asking challenging but not intimidating questions?
- Are we both clear on where the individual stands at present and where they are going?

THEORY 41 # DANIEL GOLEMAN: EMOTIONAL INTELLIGENCE

Use this to understand that a high IQ and technical expertise are not the only qualities for effective practice.

Goleman suggested that learning is not just about developing a high IQ or being technically skilled; people also need to develop their emotional intelligence. He argued that there were five key elements of emotional intelligence which are:

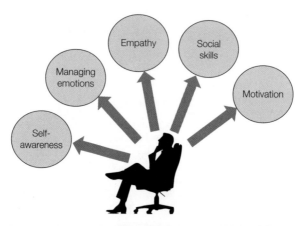

THE CHARACTERISTICS OF EACH ELEMENT ARE:

Self-awareness: Coaches must be aware of the relationship between thoughts, feelings and action. They must be able to recognise what thoughts sparked off emotions and the impact these emotions can have on themselves and others.

Managing emotions: Coaches must analyse what is behind these emotions and be able to deal with them in a positive manner.

Empathy: Coaches must be able to deal with the emotions of the person they are coaching in a positive manner. This requires the coach to be able to understand the feelings of others involved.

Social skills: Coaches need to develop quality relationships. This will have a positive effect on all involved. Knowing how and when to take the lead and when to follow is an essential social skill.

Motivation: Coaches can't always rely on external rewards to motivate others. They must support people to develop their own source of intrinsic motivators.

Goleman argued that having a high level of self-awareness and an understanding of others makes an individual a better person as well as a better coach.

HOW TO USE IT

You may have read somewhere that we're born with a huge amount of brain cells but lose thousands every day till we die. That's the bad news. The good news is it's not true: this is what Goleman refers to as 'neuromythology'. Neuroscientists claim that rather than losing cells, the brain continuously reshapes itself in line with the experiences we have (see Theories 23–25). I'm going to suggest that by persisting with positive thoughts and actions your newly reformed brain will ensure you will have a positive outlook, and will result in you naturally doing the right thing, in the right way. Of course this is speculation and so, sadly, is Goleman's theory. But doesn't it sound good and worth trying out? If you agree then here are some tips to help you:

- As a starting point, complete the emotional intelligence (EI) questionnaire devised by Goleman. It's a questionnaire, not a test. There are a number of online sites where you can access versions of this.

- Develop your self-awareness by keeping a record of any key incidents that have taken place. A simple note of what happened, why it happened, what you did and what impact it had on you and others will suffice.
  - Try to look at the incident from other people's perspectives. Although you may disagree with them, recognising that they are entitled to their views and beliefs will make you more empathetic towards them.
  - Listen carefully to what they have to say and never be afraid to re-examine your own values in light of what they have to say.
- Always try to find a win–win solution to any problem.

Although they have a popular following, both Goleman and Gardner (see Theory 39) can only speculate that their theories on intelligence are any more valid than the reliance on IQ testing. Even if you reject the theoretical rigour of Goleman's work, his model of what good emotions coaches should be displaying is still compelling.

QUESTIONS TO ASK YOURSELF

- Am I aware of the relationship between thoughts, feelings and action both in myself and the person I am coaching?
- Am I listening carefully to what they are telling me?

THEORY 42 BRUCE GRIMLEY: THE 7CS COACHING MODEL

Use this when you want a systematic coaching approach that addresses a multitude of variables that may be holding people back.

Grimley suggests that good coaching addresses a number of variables that will ensure that by the end of the coaching session, the person being coached should have achieved certain goals.

AT THE END OF COACHING, THE PERSON BEING COACHED:

is **C**lear about the objectives they are working towards;

believes that the **C**limate is right to tackle these objectives;

has the **C**apability to achieve an effective outcome;

is **C**ongruent and acts in a manner that is consistent with their feelings;

is **C**onfident in their actions;

is **C**ommitted to getting the most effective solution;

will **C**ommunicate internally and externally their intentions in line with the above.

Grimley argues that in order for the 7Cs to operate, they must be framed within an eighth C: *Courage.*

HOW TO USE IT

I like Grimley's use of the term *sailing the 7Cs* to describe the process in this model. It fits in nicely with the metaphor of people undertaking a journey.

William first came to see me for coaching after he had served a two-year jail sentence for fraud. He had been a works manager for a clothing company and realised that he was unlikely to be able to find employment in his former position. He saw self-employment as his preferred option and wanted me to act as his business coach. He had a clear vision of working with unemployed ex-offenders where he would be able to empathise with their situation. The time that he had spent in prison however had lessened his confidence and he was frequently guilty of negative self-talk.

Here are some useful tips and questions that you can ask the person who you are working with to establish the level of consciousness they have in each of the Cs:

- **Clarity**: Make these questions specific and measurable by asking: 'What is it that you want to achieve? How will you know when you have achieved it?'

- **Climate**: Relate these questions to the environment by asking: 'When is the right time to start working on the idea? How long will you devote to achieving this?'

- **Capability**: Determine whether they consider the idea is achievable by asking: 'What skills do you have that you can use to achieve your objectives?'

- **Congruency**: Discover if the proposal is compatible with their own set of values and beliefs by asking: 'What personal qualities do you have that you can use to achieve your objectives?'

- **Confidence**: Decide what their level of self-belief is by asking: 'How do you see yourself now? Where will you be in one (two or three) years' time?'

- **Commitment**: Gauge what their level of motivation is by asking: 'How much do you want this to happen?'

- **Communication**: Get a feel for the level of self-esteem they have by asking: 'What are they saying to others and themselves about their future?'

Accept that this may be a long drawn-out process. William and I worked together on his issues for six months before he felt comfortable enough in himself and had the courage to become self-employed.

QUESTIONS TO ASK YOURSELF

- Am I sure that I have covered all of the bases on this one?
- Have I covered each of the issues in sufficient depth?

THEORY 43 JOHN GRINDER: NEW BEHAVIOUR GENERATOR

Use this when you want to help someone to move from having a vision about changing to action to achieving this vision.

Grinder described the *New Behaviour Generator* (NBG) as a tool that would support someone to move from having the vision of a desired state to action to achieve this. Grinder argued that this could be achieved by someone going through a process of *mental dress rehearsal* by generating images of what the new state will look like and then linking this to some sort of visual representational process.

THE BASIC BELIEFS THAT UNDERPIN NBG ARE:

Mental mapping: People learn new behaviours by creating new mental maps of what the desired state will be.

Visualisation: The more visual and complete the mental map is, the more likely that the desired state will be achieved.

Focusing: Total focus on the outcome is the most effective and efficient way of achieving the desired state.

Resources: People possess the resources they need to achieve the desired state.

Success: Success in achieving the desired state will be a result of accessing and organising existing resources.

Grinder argues that the NBG is a technique that will help someone to achieve long-term outcomes but that the individual needs to have the ability to visualise, persistence and optimism. Grinder also suggests that an alternative use of the NBG is when the first action centres on a state to be avoided. The process remains the same for both the desired and avoidable states.

HOW TO USE IT

I have no doubt that *It's a Wonderful Life* (1946) is the greatest movie ever made! In the movie, George Bailey (played by James Stewart) has aspirations to 'do something big, something important'. Due to a series of unfortunate circumstances, George, facing bankruptcy, is driven to the edge of suicide when Clarence, an experienced coach (masquerading as George's guardian angel), intervenes. Using the

NBG, Clarence ascertains that George's desired state is that 'he had never been born'. Through using skills that only the great coaches have, Clarence transports George into a world where he hadn't been born. As George begins to see how dismal people's lives have been without him, he compares the feelings of sheer desperation that he now has with the unhappiness that he felt before doing the NBG. Ecstatic at being given one more chance at life, he finds that friends and family have rallied round to save his business, Clarence gets his wings (a special coaching award) and everyone cries. The only tragedy is that this film never won any Oscars!!

Before trying it as a coaching tool, here are some steps that you can use to apply the NBG on yourself:

- Ask, 'If I was in my desired state, what would I feel like?' Picture yourself in the desired state.
- Extend the visual images that are emerging by either associating the desired state with something similar that you may have achieved or with someone who already has the desired state who you feel comfortable modelling.
- Create a movie or mental images in which you can either be the central character in the movie or you can choose the person who you have chosen to model to be the central character. Direct the movie until you get it exactly how you want it.
- Mentally step inside the image that you have created of the central character. Describe what you would be seeing, hearing and feeling. Compare how you feel now with how you feel in the movie. If the feelings match, you are in the desired state. If they don't match then you need to question what is missing.

If by chance you have reached this point having read all of the other entries in this book, you will have appreciated my love of the movies. You don't have to be a Capra or Tarentino to be able to use the NBG: you will however need some imagination and a fair degree of belief in the approach. Don't worry if this approach is too off the wall for you, there are other approaches in the book that you can use (see Theory 21).

QUESTIONS TO ASK YOURSELF

- How good am I at visualising what my ideal state is?
- Do I feel confident enough to use the tool with the person I am coaching?

THEORY 44 **RICHARD HALE AND EILEEN HUTCHINSON: THE INSIGHT COACHING CYCLE**

Use this when you want to have a framework for supporting people to move forward.

Hale and Hutchinson claim that the benefit of using the *Insight Coaching Cycle* is that it will support the coach to achieve strength of character, transparency and the ability to develop an influential relationship with the person they are coaching based on sincere and honest dialogue. The model is based on the INSIGHT acronym.

THE CONSTITUENTS OF THE MODEL CAN BE SUMMARISED AS:

Initial assessment: This will give the coach the opportunity to elicit the core requirements for the coaching intervention.

Negotiating the coaching plan: This should cover important aspects of 'what?' 'when?' 'where?' 'how?' the intervention process will operate.

Self-development plan: This will enable the person being coached to identify areas for personal or professional development and enable the coach to discuss appropriate coaching approaches that will support the development.

Insight into own capabilities: This will encourage the individual to review their strengths and weaknesses.

Growth and personal reflection: This is an opportunity for both the person being coached and the coach to reflect on the interventions so far and evaluate what's worked well and what needs to be modified.

Hierarchy of needs: This will give both the person being coached and the coach insight into whether the needs of both parties are being met.

Testing new skills and knowledge: This will give the individual the opportunity to test new skills and knowledge and make assessments about what else needs doing.

Hale and Hutchinson claim that using this model will enable a coach to challenge perceptions, attitudes and behaviours in a relatively safe and secure manner.

HOW TO USE IT

The INSIGHT model is relatively straightforward and the process of taking an inward-looking perspective and reflection is a good way of thinking about the model. The essence of good coaching, using this model, is that the development process is two-way and depends on the two parties having absolute trust in each other. Here are some tips and insightful questions that you could ask the person you are coaching in each stage:

- Determine what the individual wants by asking: 'What specifically do you want to achieve by working with me? What counts as "success" to you? What style of coaching do you respond to best?'
- Clarify how, when and where coaching will operate by asking the individual: 'Where do you feel most comfortable learning? How do you see the client–coach relationship developing? How much time do you have to devote to coaching sessions?'
- Identify what areas for development are available by asking them: 'What are your current strengths and weaknesses? What are the opportunities and threats facing you? How can you capitalise on strengths and opportunities and eliminate weaknesses and threats?'
- Gain a deeper understanding into the individual's beliefs, values and goals by asking: 'What do you believe that you will do differently as a result of the coaching? How will this make you a better person? How will you know when you have achieved this step?'
- Confirm that the individual is on the right course by asking: 'What are you doing to make the changes happen? What are the effects that the changes have had? What do you think will change next?'
- Establish that their needs are being met by asking: 'How comfortable do you feel with what's happening to you? How would you assess your motivation to want to carry on? How will you know when you have achieved self-actualisation?'
- Confirm that the individual has achieved their desired outcome by asking: 'What are the main things that you have learned from the coaching? How do you intend applying the learning? How will you measure the effectiveness of this?'

QUESTIONS TO ASK YOURSELF

- Am I asking insightful questions?
- Am I getting honest answers to these questions?

THEORY 45 PETER HAWKINS: THE CLEAR MODEL

Use this when you want to have a systematic process for coaching that includes review of the coach's performance as well as the client's progress.

Hawkins' model is loosely based on Aristotle's claim that clarity of purpose is to:

> *First have a definite, clear practical ideal: a goal, an objective. Second have the necessary means to achieve your ends: wisdom, money, materials and methods. Thirdly, adjust all of your means to that end.*

The model is based on the CLEAR acronym and can be depicted as:

THE CONSTITUENTS OF THE MODEL CAN BE SUMMARISED AS:

Contracting: This is where the coach clarifies what outcomes the individual wants to achieve from the coaching and establishes the scope of the coaching and the ground rules for working together.

Listening: This is where the coach listens actively and with empathy to the person being coached in order to gain an understanding of their situation and personal insight into the problem.

Exploration: This stage consists of two elements: (a) helping the individual to understand what impact the current situation is having on them: (b) challenging the individual to think through the possibilities of what can be achieved.

Action: This is where the coach supports the person being coached to choose the most appropriate way forward.

Review: This stage consists of two elements: (a) reviewing the individual's progress – what decisions have been made and what impact has this had on them? (b) reviewing the coach's input in the process – what helped or hindered the individual's progress and what they would like to see done differently in future coaching sessions?

HOW TO USE IT

The principles of transparency and feedback are a good way of looking at the CLEAR model. The essence of good coaching, using this model, is the desire for feedback from the client on what's working and if necessary adapting the coaching approach before committing to further action. Here are some useful points to bear in mind in each stage:

- The rules for effective coaching are important for both the coach and the person being coached. Have a set of ground rules that you both subscribe to. Don't impose these: determine them together as this will engender a sense of ownership and commitment by both parties.

- Listen attentively throughout the session to what the individual has to say. Make sure they are in no doubt that you are fully aware of what they are saying. Demonstrate this by paraphrasing what they have said and summarising your understanding.

- Find out what's going on in the individual's world at the moment. You're not their therapist but don't confine your questions to their professional world. Things may be happening in their personal lives that affect their ability to learn.

- Don't give advice but do support them to reach their own conclusions about what they need to do next and how they need to set about it.

- Build in time to reflect on what's been achieved and readjust your input for the next session if necessary. Make sure the feedback you get is an honest appraisal and that you respond to their feedback in a positive manner.

QUESTIONS TO ASK YOURSELF

- Have we set ground rules that we are both comfortable with?
- Have I encouraged the person I am coaching to reflect on where they are at present and where they want to get to?
- Am I eliciting feedback about my performance as a coach and acting on this?

JON KABAT-ZINN: MINDFULNESS

Use this when you want to coach people to deal effectively with stress.

Although *mindfulness* is based on some of the principles of Buddhism, it was the work of Kabat-Zinn that popularised it as a coaching tool. According to Kabat-Zinn, *mindfulness* is about dealing with thoughts in a detached, de-centred and non-judgemental manner. This can be depicted as:

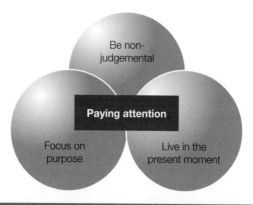

EACH OF THESE CHARACTERISTICS CAN BE SUMMARISED AS:

Be non-judgemental: Don't allow your own goals and values to affect your judgement on what's happening to the person you are coaching.

Focus on purpose: Learn to manage the discomfort of uncertainty. Don't get side-tracked when things don't go right. Stay focused on the coaching task in hand.

Live in the present moment: Learn to slow down, ignore negative brain chatter about the coaching and experience the event for what it is.

Central to Kabat-Zinn's theory is the notion of using meditative techniques to stay in the body and to observe what thoughts are going on in the mind but not to identify with them. This, according to Kabat-Zinn, requires acceptance that our minds have a life of their own.

HOW TO USE IT

Someone once told me that if you can't find 20 minutes to meditate each day, find an hour. Most people accept that taking time over their hygiene (showering, brushing teeth etc.) or exercising is essential, but ignore the care and attention needed for their greatest asset – their mind. The mind can be the source of happiness or despair, creativity or self-destruction, problem-solving or problem-making.

Have you ever seen John Cleese's wonderful portrayal of the hotel owner, Basil Fawlty, in the BBC television series *Fawlty Towers*? Basil seems to launch from one crisis to another as his plans seem destined to fail. In one hilarious but also, to my mind, tragic episode, Basil attempts to raise the status of his hotel with a gourmet evening. Needless to say, everything goes wrong and he ends up berating and thrashing his broken-down car with a tree trunk.

If this sounds familiar then, like Basil, I suspect that every time you try to catch a bit of down time, something happens that only you can attend to. Who are you kidding? Are you really that indispensable that you are the only person you can trust to get things right? If you were asked to be Basil's coach, what would you do?

- Well, you could start by making sure that Basil sharpens his focus. Get him to look at his daily routine and list the things that are important and the things that are not important. Get him then to go down the important list and separate the things that are urgent from the things that are non-urgent.

- Now get him to deal with all issues that are important and urgent. Make sure that he sets aside some time for the things that are important but non-urgent. Get him to delegate the things that are non-important but urgent. Finally get him to look at the things that are neither important nor urgent and ask him why he's doing these things.

- By now, Basil should have created at least 20 minutes for meditating. This should help him to cultivate a different state of mind which hopefully will give him a different perspective on everyday life.

- If you've been successful then Basil will start to learn to experience the present moment as it really is and to develop the ability to step away from his habitual knee-jerk reaction to events. He will start to see things as they really are and respond to them wisely rather than on auto-pilot.

If you were Basil's coach and turned him from the manic hotel owner into the genial host then you must shoulder the blame for the premature end of one of the funniest shows ever to be televised. Sorry, I can't forgive you for that!

QUESTION TO ASK YOURSELF

- Have I convinced the person I am coaching of the need to find at least 20 minutes each day for reflective thinking?

THEORY 47 MAX LANDSBERG: THE TAO OF COACHING

Use this when you want to increase your own effectiveness as a manager by helping others to develop and grow.

Landsberg argues that coaching involves giving feedback, motivation and effective questioning. He claims that the coach's main role is to recognise the individual's readiness to undertake a particular task in terms of both their *will* and *skill*. He suggests that coaching approaches will depend on the extent of *skill* and *will* along the following lines:

Source: Landsberg, M. (2003) *The Tao of Coaching*. London: Profile Books.

COACHES SHOULD DEVELOP A GAME PLAN THAT INCLUDES:

Setting the context: This will involve: diagnosis of the levels of skill and will; being explicit about the approach to be undertaken; building trust in the relationship; finding out what excites the individual; and painting a compelling vision about what can be achieved.

Providing ongoing coaching: This will involve choosing the most appropriate intervention measure which could be: substantive and structured sessions lasting 20 to 60 minutes; brief discussions on performance of 5 to 10 minutes; or very brief but frequent bouts of feedback.

Concluding effectively: This will involve: reflection on what's been learned; obtaining feedback on your performance as a coach; and deciding on what happens next.

Landsberg describes coaching as a dynamic interaction that doesn't rely on a one-way flow of telling or instruction. In this respect he claims that coaches can also develop from the experience.

HOW TO USE IT

With some books, you get excited by the title only to be disappointed by the contents. This isn't the case with *The Tao of Coaching* (Profile Books, 2003). The book mixes some interesting theory and models with the story of an individual's experiences as a coach. Here are a few tips, taken from these experiences:

- Firstly, in setting the context make it part of your coaching habit that you don't dive headfirst into suggesting the individual does this or does that. Telling without asking is bad karma (am I mixing my cultures here?). Do your background research into the levels of the individual's *skills* and *will*. Ask what they already have to offer in terms of knowledge and ability and how well motivated they are to develop further. Never be afraid of sharing your own strengths and limitations with the person you are coaching. This will be a very powerful way of building trust in the relationship. Once you have developed this trust you can elicit what really excites the individual and how to pitch your vision of what's possible.

- Once you have established the context, you need to agree on which coaching interventions work best for you and the individual. You need to take into account the logistics of the situation. Frequent one-hour sessions may not be feasible if you both have other important functions to fulfil. Brief comments in passing however may not achieve anything substantial. Ask the individual what works best for them and see if you can fit it in with your other routines. A small number of substantive sessions backed up with occasional discussions and regular feedback on performance will be the ideal.

- You won't want the coaching experience to just fizzle out, leaving both you and the individual feeling a sense of dissatisfaction with what's taken place. Try to get effective closure. As well as improving the performance of the individual, you'll want your own self-esteem and reputation as a coach to grow as a result of the intervention. Get them to reflect on what they've learned and what contribution they feel you have made to this. Always ask the individual what they plan to do next.

QUESTIONS TO ASK YOURSELF

- Have I taken enough care and attention in finding out the desired outcomes for both the individual and the organisation?
- Am I willing to accept feedback on my own performance as a coach from the person I am coaching?

THEORY 48 # DAVID LANE AND SARAH CORRIE: PURPOSE, PERSPECTIVES AND PROCESS

Use this when you want to structure coaching in terms of a journey.

Lane and Corrie suggested that their *purpose, perspectives and process* model would assist coaches by enabling them to have a clear purpose for the coaching, a framework of underlying perspectives that inform the coach's approach and a set of structures that enable both the coach and the individual to act effectively.

The three constituents of the model can be summarised in terms of the coach and the individual going on a journey asking key questions.

THE KEY QUESTIONS ASKED ARE:

Purpose: Where are we going and why? Establish exactly what it is that the person being coached wants to achieve.

Perspectives: What will inform our journey? Find out what experiences both parties have of coaching and how this will influence what happens during coaching.

Process: How will we get there? Determine the most productive ways of working together.

Lane and Corrie argue that the model can be used for either one single part of the journey or the complete journey. They claim that using the model will help the coach to understand the needs of the person they are coaching, develop a rapport with them and identify ways of working together.

HOW TO USE IT

This is a very simple model that can have quite profound implications for the coach. Here's a true story:

> Harold was a skilled engineer who, like many of his contemporaries, was experiencing difficulties in the early 1970s in finding work in engineering. I had trained as an employment coach and was working with Harold to help him find work. I knew what was right for him and convinced him to switch from working in engineering to the service

sector where there were jobs. I was notified of a job as a shop floor attendant with a major DIY store. I badgered Harold into applying. He went for an interview. He didn't get the job and shortly afterwards committed suicide.

I felt that I had built up an excellent relationship with him and that he trusted my judgement. Where I realise now that I went wrong was that I assumed the dominant role in the relationship: it was my solution to the problem not his. Here are some tips to help avoid coaching situations getting out of hand:

- Discuss the purpose of the interaction. Find out exactly what the individual wants to achieve. Take time getting to know one another. Draw up a picture of the person who you are working with through conversation. Establish rapport and identify areas of mutual interest.

- Find out what previous experience they have had of being coached and how they felt about this. Share some of your own experiences of coaching or being coached. Remember that you both come into the relationship with individual backgrounds, experiences and expertise that will shape behaviour.

- Find out a way of working together. Describe what you feel you can and can't do. Don't build up a level of expectation of support that you can't provide. Discuss what opportunities and options do exist and the most useful kind of assistance you can provide. Share your perspectives of their needs and limitations candidly.

Telling the person who you are working with what to do may not be the best thing for them. Supporting them to decide for themselves will give them ownership of the issue.

QUESTIONS TO ASK YOURSELF

- Do I fully understand what the individual wants from the coaching experience?
- Have we agreed on how we'll work together to get the most out of the coaching experience?

THEORY 49 ANGUS MCLEOD: THE STEPPPA MODEL

Use this when you want to have a systematic process that ensures motivated plans lead to achievement of targets.

McLeod claims that his model contains the prime elements that help the coach to be sure that their client has reached a motivated strategy for success. The model is based on the STEPPPA acronym.

THE CONSTITUENTS OF THE MODEL CAN BE SUMMARISED AS:

Subject: This is where the coach checks that the issues being addressed are within the boundaries of the individual–coach relationship.

Target objective: This is where the coach assesses whether the target being set by the person being coached is realistic.

Emotional context: This is where the coach assesses whether the individual has sufficient emotional attachment to the issue to want to do something about it.

Perception and target re-evaluation: This is where the coach aims to widen the individual's conscious perception of their issues and targets.

Plan: This is an opportunity for both the individual and the coach to reflect on the interventions so far and evaluate what's worked well and what needs to be modified.

Pace: This is where the individual and coach decide on whether things are going according to schedule or whether the timeline for achievement needs to be re-worked.

Adapt or act: This is where both parties review the plan and make necessary adjustments before committing to action.

McLeod suggests that the steps may not always follow the sequence outlined above but he adds that every step is important and that it may be risky to miss any of them out completely.

HOW TO USE IT

The principle of building up the process step-by-step is a good way of thinking about the STEPPPA model. The essence of good coaching, using this model, is the rigour that underpins the process in terms of laying the foundations, reflecting on what's working and, if necessary, adapting the plan before committing to action. Here are some useful points to bear in mind in each stage:

- Be aware that the person you are coaching will bring a variety of issues with them to the coaching session. Some of these will be planned in advance, others may arise as the session is underway. You need to check that the issues are things that you are contracted to deal with. If not, explain to the individual that you are uncomfortable dealing with the issue and suggest they need to seek other help.

- You may find that some individuals have ambitious targets but lack the motivation or confidence to achieve them. Don't be afraid of challenging them if their targets are unrealistic. Also be aware that target objectives will have to fit in with organisational needs.

- Get the person you are coaching to give an indication of how much emotional attachment they have to the issue by asking them to rate this on a scale of nought (low attachment) to ten (high attachment). Encourage them to extend their conscious perception of the issue and to develop a wider and clearer view of what needs to be done.

- Make sure that you, and the person you are coaching, reflect on whether the targets set are achievable, that the strategy for implementation is feasible and that you both have considered the wider implications for colleagues and the organisation. When you reflect, discuss whether the pace of coaching is too quick or too slow. You may wish to do this alongside the planning stage or even earlier if appropriate. It may not matter when you make these considerations relative to planning as long as you do it.

- Finally, be aware that both of you have invested time and effort into the process and may want to move on. Also be aware that motivation is a variable force and their perception of what's been achieved may be affected by this. Constantly checking the individual's perception and emotion towards the issue will ensure they have sufficient commitment to addressing the issue before moving on.

QUESTIONS TO ASK YOURSELF

- Are we operating within boundaries that we both feel comfortable in?
- Does the person I am coaching have sufficient emotional commitment to achieving their goal?
- Have we built in sufficient time to reflect on progress and are we willing to act on this?

THEORY 50 # ALEC MCPHEDRAN: THE GENIUS MODEL

Use this when you want to have a coaching framework for developing creative people.

McPhedran claimed that the *GENIUS model* was a coaching tool that would push and develop ambition and creativity for creative people by working with the individual to turn their imagination and aspiration into an inspiring and exciting reality. The model can be depicted as:

Goals   **E**nergy   **N**urture   **I**nhibitors   **U**topia   **S**teps

THE CONSTITUENTS OF THE MODEL CAN BE SUMMARISED AS:

Goals: The model incorporates three types of goals that need to be set in order to provide the coach with consistency and focus to make things happen. The goals are: (a) the aspirational goal of the coaching contract; (b) the goals that need to be achieved by the end of a coaching session; and (c) the goals that need to be actioned before the start of the next coaching session.

Energy: Once the goals have been set, the coach and individual need to discuss if the individual has the energy to achieve the goals. This is where the coach assesses whether the target being set by the individual is realistic. Setting unrealistic goals will have an adverse effect on energy.

Nurture: Once the goals and energy levels needed to achieve them have been established, the coach needs to nurture the individual. This will involve questioning, listening and encouraging creative thinking and risk taking.

Inhibitors: This is where the coach and the individual review the factors that prevent achievement of their desired outcome. This stage aims to widen the individual's conscious perception of their issues and targets.

Utopia: By this stage the individual will have a vision of their ideal state.

Steps: This is where the individual and the coach review the plan and make necessary adjustments before committing to action.

McPhedran admitted that the model may not be perfect for some but argued that the essence of creative coaching was turning the individual's imagination and aspiration into an inspiring and exciting reality.

HOW TO USE IT

This is probably the least known but, arguably, one of the most inspiring of the coaching models in this part of the book. McPhedran works as a talent coach in the media communication industries and admits that he recognised that his task as a coach wasn't about imparting his wisdom but about supporting the people he was coaching to develop their own ideas and solutions to problems. Here are a few tips to help you use the model:

- The first step is to set the goals for the coaching. These will fall into one of three categories. For aspirational goals, make sure these are ground-breaking and highly ambitious. For sessional goals determine what the individual will have achieved by the end of the session. For action goals, agree what steps the individual will take before the next session to move them one step closer to achieving their aspirational goal. Always look to make these goals specific, measurable, achievable, realistic and timebound (see Theories 11–13).

- Make sure that there is not a massive gap between the individual's desire to achieve something and their energy levels to get this done. Get them to rate their energy level during each coaching session and to compare this with the levels in previous sessions. Get them to discuss why this may have risen or fallen and what they can do about it.

- Build in sufficient time to reflect on both progress and process and make any necessary adjustments to the coaching plan.

Nurturing creativity is not about telling the individual what to do, it's about working with the individual to support them to increase their self-awareness of what options are available to them and what needs to be done to close the gap between where they are at present and where they need to be.

QUESTIONS TO ASK YOURSELF

- Have we set goals that are aspirational, achievable and actionable?
- Does the individual have the energy and commitment to achieve these goals?
- Does the individual have a vision of what they can achieve?
- Have we set aside sufficient time to review progress?

THEORY 51

ERIC PARSLOE AND MONIKA WRAY: THE SEVEN GOLDEN RULES OF SIMPLICITY

Use this when you want a simple set of rules for a coaching process.

Parsloe and Wray argued that the quality of outcomes from coaching activities were dependent on the quality of the relationship between the people concerned. They developed the *Seven Golden Rules of Simplicity* as a process for managing a coaching relationship.

THESE CAN BE SUMMARISED AS:

Success comes from doing simple things consistently: Don't make the coaching programme too elaborate or dictated to by rules or unrealistic expectations.

Make sure you make time to meet: Busy coaches or managers don't always find the time to meet the people they are coaching. The converse can also be true.

Keep it brief: Allocate sufficient time to cover the points you both need to cover. Some situations however may prove stressful if rushed, so be flexible.

Stick to the basic process: Have an agreed way of operating and stick to it.

Adopt an 'ask, not tell' habit: The 80–20 rule (see Theory 68) is useful here – 80 per cent asking questions and 20 per cent giving answers.

Remember, it's all about learning: Coaching should not just be about directing but about encouraging self-growth. Regular and on-going coaching should be part of the organisation's learning culture (see Theories 59–60).

Expect to gain yourself: It's not only the person being coached but also the coach who will benefit from a well-run coaching experience

Parsloe and Wray are strong advocates of the principle that helping people to learn to manage their own learning is the underpinning concept of good coaching. They argue that, although coaching isn't a new activity, what is new is the extent to which the power of coaching has been harnessed to meet the challenge of ever-increasing needs to learn things in new ways.

HOW TO USE IT

When I left full-time education in the mid 1970s and joined the Department of Employment, I was introduced to the concept of 'sitting with Nellie'. I never actually met Nellie but there were lots of Bills and Toms and Marys who would always be willing to show me how to complete a claim for unemployment benefit and where to file it. I probably wasn't aware of it at the time but this represented on-the-job coaching. What I realise now is that although I appreciated the time they gave me in showing me how to do things, I was being taught their methods of doing things in their own inimitable styles of coaching me.

Here are some tips to help you keep the coaching approach simple but meaningful:

- Don't over-complicate the role or erect unrealistic or unnecessary barriers and expectations.
- Be aware that most coaching schemes fail because the busy coach doesn't make sufficient time available to meet with the client and vice versa.
- If time is precious there's no point in wasting it. Allocate sufficient time to deal with the issue. Meeting regularly and briefly is better than meeting only occasionally and spending too much time on the issue.
- Have a process that involves: pre-session preparation, a commitment to act and agreed follow-up. This will ensure coaching sessions are focused, structured and well time-managed.
- Develop an 'ask, not tell' habit. Good coaching is less 'hands-on' and more of a 'hands-off' technique. A useful habit to work on is to have 80 per cent asking questions in any coaching session and 20 per cent giving answers.
- Constantly remind the people you are coaching that coaching is all about learning and point out the real-life benefits of this. This is a good approach to gaining commitment to the session.
- Accept that learning is not a one-way process. The individual, the coach and their organisation should all derive benefit from effective coaching. Never be afraid to express self-interests when coaching someone.

QUESTIONS TO ASK YOURSELF

- Do I make sure that I always point out the real-life benefits of the coaching?
- Am I making sure that I ask at least four times more questions than I give out answers?
- Do I make sure that I am also gaining benefit from the coaching?

THEORY 52   JENNY ROGERS: THE SIX PRINCIPLES OF COACHING

Use this when you want a basic set of principles to support you to coach at all levels within an organisation.

Rogers claims that coaching is a partnership of equals whose aim is to achieve increased and sustainable effectiveness through focused activity. She suggests that coaching raises self-awareness and identifies choices. She offers her *Six Principles of Coaching* model as a process for achieving this.

THE SIX PRINCIPLES CAN BE SUMMARISED AS:

The client is resourceful: This principle is based on the belief that only the person being coached knows the full story about their predicament and only they can actually implement the action. In that respect they have the resources to be able to solve their problems.

The coach's role is to help the client to develop this resourcefulness: A coach's role is not to give advice because this suggests they know what's best for the individual which may lead to dependency on the coach.

Coaching addresses the whole person: This is about taking into account the person's past, present and future lives and involves both their work and personal circumstances.

The client sets the agenda: When the person being coached sets the agenda, they feel a sense of inclusion and empowerment and are more likely to contribute towards planning, problem-solving and decision-making.

The coach and the client are equals: Both work together as equals in a relationship based on total respect and trust.

Coaching is about change and action: Essentially, people seek coaching because they want something to change and generally want to be more effective.

The philosophy underpinning Roger's model is that the core purpose of coaching is to increase self-awareness, to make choices explicit and to close the gap between what the client is currently doing and what they are capable of doing.

HOW TO USE IT

Although much of what Rogers advocated relates to organisational coaching, her principles can be equally applied to coaching individuals. Here are some steps to help you apply the six principles:

- Make sure that the person you are coaching has sufficient information and resources to achieve their desired outcome. If not find out what you can do to help them get it but don't spoon-feed them with it. Remember you can offer useful information but it must always be the individual's choice whether or not to use it.

- Never give advice. This implies that you know better than them, that they therefore are lesser people which in turn may lead to them become dependent on you. Of course you're not their coach for nothing and they clearly want to learn from you but do this by asking challenging questions and getting them to reach their conclusions about what to do next.

- Although you're not their therapist, there may be issues that they have to deal with, that require you to look beyond the immediate circumstances; personal as well as professional. You may feel uncomfortable about this and will need to know what your boundaries are. Don't duck these issues but have the sense if necessary to signpost them to others who may have more expertise in dealing with the issue.

- There should be no hidden agendas. It's the individual's role to set the agenda for the coaching and your role to respond to this. If you feel that the agenda poses difficulties for you to deal with as their coach, tell them how you feel and discuss what alternatives are possible.

- Work together with the person you are coaching on an equal footing. You may be coaching a junior member of staff or a senior executive. You may be getting double or half the salary of the person you are coaching. None of this is relevant when coaching, and the relationship should be based on the trust and respect that should underpin all colleague-to-colleague relationships.

- Appreciate that the individual is being coached by you because they want to improve on some aspect of their work. Your role is to support the individual by increasing their self-awareness of what options are available to them and what needs to be done to close the gap between where they are at present and where they want to be.

QUESTIONS TO ASK YOURSELF

- Have I created a high level of respect and trust in the relationship?
- Are we approaching the coaching on an equal footing?
- Have I allowed the individual to set the agenda?

THEORY 53   # VIRGINIA SATIR: ANCHORING AND SELF-COACHING

Use this when you want to help someone or yourself to be able to control thoughts and feelings.

Although, I have attributed this entry to Satir, it was the work of Amos Tversky and Daniel Kahneman that introduced the notion of *anchoring* into the public domain.

Satir describes *anchoring* as a process whereby something visual, audible or tactile can act as a stimulus to trigger a required response. She explains that anchors can be conscious or subconscious, positive or negative, and either occur naturally or are constructed. The anchoring process can be depicted as:

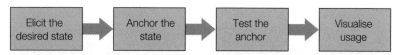

| Elicit the desired state | Anchor the state | Test the anchor | Visualise usage |

EACH ELEMENT IN THE PROCESS CAN BE SUMMARISED AS:

Elicit the desired state: Visualise exactly what it is that you want to be/do in the desired state.

Anchor the state: Select a stimulus (visual, audible or tactile or any combination of these) that you can associate with how you will feel when you are in the desired state.

Test the anchor: Disassociate from the anchored state and think about or do something totally unconnected with the desired state. Then return back to it.

Envisage a time when it will be used: Imagine a situation when you want to experience the desired state. Use the anchor to check that it will be sufficient to deal with the situation.

Satir points out that you can also use this technique to eliminate old and unwanted states that are causing negative feelings and/or unwanted behaviours.

HOW TO USE IT

Here are some tips on how to help you, or the person who you are coaching, to develop meaningful anchors:

- Find somewhere nice and quiet with no distractions.
- Select something (touch, feel, sight, smell etc.) or a combination of things that you intend to use as the anchor (I find that pressing my thumb and forefinger together works well for me and isn't so conspicuous in company).
- Think of something that generates warm or positive thoughts. Step back into those thoughts and visualise how you felt. Like the volume and colour controls on your television set, start to turn up the intensity of your senses in this visualisation. Just as you begin to reach peak intensity, activate your anchor.
- Return to your current state. See if the anchor is taking you to your desired state. If it is then you have successfully constructed your anchor. If not, then try it another four or five times, increasing the intensity of your senses each time. If it still isn't working try a different anchor and repeat the process.

You may be lucky and hit on an anchor straight away or you may have to keep repeating the process till you get there. The more acute the sensory experience, the less repetition you'll need. I promise you that persevering with this tool will be worthwhile. You will be surprised at where you can use this technique: for example building up your confidence when giving an important presentation, or calming your nerves when at the dentists, or not losing your temper when the person with the biggest bag of popcorn in the world sits behind you in the cinema.

QUESTIONS TO ASK YOURSELF

- Have I been able to find an anchor that works for me?
- Have I been able to find an anchor that works for the person I am coaching?

JOHN SWELLER: COGNITIVE LOAD THEORY

Use this when you don't want to overload the person you are coaching with too much information.

Sweller described *cognitive load* as the amount of information that working memory can hold at any one time. He claimed that, since working memory has a limited capacity, coaches should avoid overloading the client with additional activities that do not contribute towards achievement of the task in hand. There are four key elements to *cognitive load theory* that can be summarised relative to coaching.

THE FOUR KEY ELEMENTS CAN BE SUMMARISED AS:

Measure expertise: This is where the coach assesses the level of skills and knowledge of the person they are coaching and adapts their coaching to reflect this.

Reduce the problem space: Problem space is defined as the gap between the current situation and the desired goal. Overload of working memory may occur if this is too large.

Reduce split-attention effect: Split attention occurs when the individual's attention is divided between a multitude of sources of information delivered in the same format (auditory or visual).

Capitalise on auditory and visual channels within working memory: Auditory and visual communication have their own working memory spaces. The cognitive load on each space can be reduced by the coach combining auditory and visual instructions.

Sweller argued that a pre-coaching session that involves more basic or prerequisite skills or knowledge before the main coaching session would help clients to establish schemas that extend their working memory and increase their capacity to follow more complex coaching instructions.

HOW TO USE IT

Using cognitive load theory will help you design coaching sessions that help the people you are coaching to learn more effectively by reducing the demands on their working memory. Here are some useful points to bear in mind in order to reduce the level of cognitive overload:

■ Adapt your input to reflect the level of knowledge or expertise of the people who you are coaching. You can do this by formal methods such as written tests or training needs analyses. Of course you could simply ask them. Once you have a clear picture of the level people are at, make sure that you set objectives that are compatible with this (see Theories 11–13).

■ If the gap between the level they are at and where they need to be is too great, you should break down what needs to be done in a series of bite-sizable steps. Make sure that, if you do this, you allow them the opportunity to consolidate what's been learned before moving on to the next step.

■ Don't bombard them with an array of visual or auditory information all at the same time. You may have heard the expression 'death by PowerPoint': this happens when the coach overdoes the visual aids to such an extent that the person being coached is unable to absorb essential information because their attention is attracted to other less important images. Similarly, you should avoid talking about an important topic if there is extraneous noise going on such as other people talking or music playing in the background

■ You can however mix auditory and visual aids as these have their own discrete memory spaces. Directing people's attention to a diagram while talking about it will not create cognitive overload.

Remember that the information you give out to the people you are coaching remains in their working memory until it has been processed sufficiently to pass into their long-term memory vaults. Read Theories 23–25 to get a better understanding of how the brain processes and retains information.

QUESTIONS TO ASK YOURSELF

■ Will the material I have prepared create cognitive overload?

■ How can I prepare aids that will support learning rather than hinder it?

THEORY 55 | # JOHN WHITMORE: THE GROW MODEL

Use this when you want to help people to make better decisions and solve problems related to their career.

Whitmore suggests that the GROW model is a simple but powerful way of structuring a coaching session. He likens it to thinking about planning a journey in which you decide where you are going (the **G**oal), establish where you are at present (the **R**eality), explore the various routes (the **O**ptions) and be committed to reaching your destination (the **W**ill to succeed). The model can be depicted as:

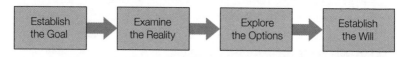

THE CONSTITUENTS OF THE MODEL CAN BE SUMMARISED AS:

Establish the goal: Look at the behaviour that the other person wants to change and express this in terms of a goal that they want to achieve.

Examine the current reality: Encourage the individual to avoid trying to solve problems before considering where they are at present.

Explore the options: After exploring the reality, turn the person's attention to determining what is possible.

Establish the will: Now that the options are clear get the individual to commit to specific actions in order to move forward towards achieving their goal.

Whitmore stresses the importance of the coach not considering themselves to be an expert in the other person's predicament and not trying to solve their problems for them. He describes the ultimate role of the coach as being a facilitator who helps the person to select the best options.

HOW TO USE IT

The GROW model is possibly the most widely used of all of the models. It is relatively straightforward and the metaphor of organic growth is a good way of thinking about the model. The essence of good coaching, using this model, is asking good questions. Here are some useful tips and questions that you could ask your client in each stage:

- Make sure that their goal is specific, measurable, achievable, realistic and time-bound. Ask them: 'How does this relate to your career objectives? When will you know that you have achieved your goal? How confident are you that you can achieve this objective? What is a realistic schedule for achieving the objective?'

- Don't allow them to start coming up with solutions before they've even considered where they stand at present. Ask: 'What is happening to you now? How do you feel about what is happening? What have you been doing to date to address the issue? How does this issue impact on other issues you are facing?'

- Avoid coming up with the options. Remember these may be your options as to how you would tackle the situation. You should however get the individual to consider the viability of each option by asking: 'What are the possible repercussions of adopting this option? What could you do if something goes wrong? What factors do you need to consider when weighing up an option?'

- Having explored the options, you now need to get the individual to commit to specific courses of action by asking: 'What will you do next? When will you do it by? How will you know that it's been done?'

Notice that all of the questions asked are open questions. Try to avoid asking closed questions that just require a 'yes' or 'no' answer. Make sure that when the person you are coaching responds to your question that you listen in an attentive and non-judgemental manner. In this respect your body language may be more important than what you actually say.

QUESTIONS TO ASK YOURSELF

- Have I made absolutely sure that the individual appreciates their present situation before embarking on any developments?
- Have I got them to commit to action?

SUMMARY OF PART 2

In Part 2, I have put together a toolbox for managers, coaches, mentors or teachers to use when working with people. Which tool you decide to use will depend on the person, the issue and the context in which you are working with them.

I chose to present the tools in alphabetical order, rather than look for alternative classifications, because the tools can be used in any coaching situation and I didn't want to steer you towards any particular model. It will also help you if you have heard about a particular model and want to find out more about it.

The key points to emerge from this part of the book are:

- It's important to understand how a person's behaviour, capabilities, beliefs and values affect how they respond to coaching.
- People filter out information that may not be relevant to them.
- A good working relationship is essential for building commitment to performance improvement.
- Encourage people to look on challenge as an opportunity not a threat.
- Encourage people to develop positive self-talk.
- Don't be afraid of challenging people if it's in their best interests.
- Tell people that failing at something doesn't mean they are a failure.
- Your sense of reality may not be the same as other people who you are working with.
- You can never really know how another person is feeling because you cannot really get into their mind.
- Support people to develop their own solutions to problems.
- Don't overload the person you are coaching with too much information.
- If you can visualise it you can do it.

PART 3

COACHING THE ORGANISATION FOR BETTER PERFORMANCE

INTRODUCTION

I n this part of the book, the emphasis is on you as the coach working with an organisation, either as a manager in the organisation or as a business coach or consultant brought in to deal with a specific issue. I've chosen a number of aspects of organisational behaviour that reflect the issues within an organisation that will have an impact on their performance. I have selected just three theories in each of the categories that I feel will offer an interesting perspective on the subject and more importantly guidance as to how, as the coach, you can support them to be better performers.

Before looking at specific aspects of organisational management, I want to cover some theories relating to the concept of leadership and the *learning organisation* which may give an indication of how the organisation will respond to your coaching. It may seem strange describing organisational development in terms of such a humanistic function as learning. Learning however is about behaviour modification, it is organic and does grow and develop and, if we accept the view that the organisation is made up of the people who work there and not just bricks and mortar, then we begin to see the relevance of the term *learning organisation*.

The sections that follow cover theories which will help you to understand more about:

- **Leadership**: Why leaders are important to the organisation.
- **Competition**: Why the organisation needs to learn in order to be better than their competitors.
- **Culture**: Why the organisation is what it is.
- **Planning**: Why the organisation does what it does.
- **Quality**: Why the organisation needs to do better.
- **Transition**: Why the organisation needs to respond to change.
- **Teamworking**: Why people in the organisation need to work together.

More importantly it will equip you with the knowledge and skills to be able to function more effectively as a coach within the organisation.

SECTION 1

COACHING ORGANISATIONAL LEADERS

INTRODUCTION

In recent years there has been a change in people's perception of leadership and management. The dominant view for many years was that leadership was an integral part of the manager's role. Bennis and Nanus introduced a different model which can be summarised as: 'Managers do things right whereas leaders do the right thing.' In this respect, I want to draw the distinction between the two functions in terms of:

- leaders setting new directions and *initiating* the vision;
- managers concentrating on operations and *interpreting* the vision.

It's important here that I emphasise that there are aspects of management that involve leading (around 20 per cent) and aspects of leadership that involve managing (around 20 per cent). Obviously this percentage will vary depending on the respective role expectation and size of the organisation.

This section in the book is written for managers who have a specific leadership function in that they have to analyse the demands of a situation, select the most appropriate response to these demands and have the right people in place to see the response through. This may seem a tall order for some junior or middle managers. There is a plethora of books and courses available for leaders to support them with the theories that underpin leadership but few of these can teach a manager how to create a vision for the future of the organisation, how to take calculated risks and launch a new product or service or how to exercise and feel comfortable with power. This is where coaching can play a big part in supporting the manager when they have to make difficult decisions and for developing essential skills such as making sound judgements and being able to communicate effectively.

The three entries chosen in this section reflect some of the most influential theories on the subject of leadership. I wanted entries that introduced a new way of thinking about leadership and that reflected leadership development in terms of a journey of discovery.

THEORY 56   JOHN ADAIR: ACTION-CENTRED LEADERSHIP

Use this when you want to show leaders how to balance the needs of the task, the team and the individual.

Adair argued that leaders must continually balance out the needs of the task, the team and the individual. His model for *action-centred leadership* is made up of three overlapping circles representing each of the three leadership responsibilities. These can be described as:

- **Task**: This involves goal-setting, planning, allocating work and resources, setting deadlines, monitoring and controlling progress.
- **Team**: This involves taking steps to ensure the integration of effort, encouraging co-operation within the team, resolving conflicts and developing team spirit.
- **Individual**: This includes meeting any training, coaching, mentoring or counselling needs of the individual members of the team

With this model at the heart of the leader's role, Adair outlined eight key functions that leaders were responsible for.

THESE CAN BE SUMMARISED AS:

Defining the task: Setting objectives that are clear, specific, measurable and achievable.

Planning: Looking at ways of achieving the task and having a contingency plan in place in case of problems.

Briefing the team: Creating a positive outlook within the team and a sense that the task can be done.

Controlling activities: Getting maximum results from minimum resources.

Monitoring: Evaluating results and looking for performance improvements.

Motivating individuals: Using extrinsic motivators such as rewards and incentives and intrinsic motivators such as pride and self-esteem to get the best out of individuals.

Organising people: Making sure there is good time management and that personal development needs are being met.

Role modelling: Setting a good example to everyone.

Adair claimed that his model challenged conventional models of leadership by showing that good leadership was something that could be coached rather than being a trait that the leader possessed.

HOW TO USE IT

Here are some tips to help you get the leader to think about their responsibilities in terms of task, team and individuals:

- Get the leader to think about what task-oriented, goal-seeking activities they have been involved in. Get them to analyse how effective they have been in completing the task and what factors affected the outcome. If the task wasn't completed successfully but team and individual performance were exemplary then it could be that there were problems in defining the objectives or planning how to achieve them. Get them to check if objectives were clear, specific, measurable and realistic. Ask them if they had a contingency plan in place if things were going wrong with the task (see Theories 65–67).

- Get the leader to think about what team-related activities they carry out. Get them to focus on steps they have taken to integrate and co-ordinate activities and create a good team spirit. If they have done this but the team are still underperforming then it could be that there is the wrong mix of people in the team (see Theory 74) or that the individuals haven't developed yet as a team (see Theory 75).

- Get the leader to think about what they have done to develop individuals within the team. Get them to describe what training, coaching or mentoring they have used, the purpose behind using this and the outcomes. Get them to review how they motivate individuals to get the best out of them (see Theories 5–7) and consider what impact they have as a role model (see Theory 22).

- Warn the leader that there may be a clash between the needs of the task, team or individual. If this happens, the leader will need to prioritise based on what is best for the organisation in the long term. If, in doing this, the leader finds that they are neglecting one or more of their other responsibilities then advise them that they must restore the balance over a period of time.

QUESTION TO ASK YOURSELF

- Have I convinced the leader of the need for a balanced approach across the three areas?

THEORY 57 BERNARD BASS: TRANSFORMATIONAL LEADERSHIP

Use this when you want to impress on the leader the importance of good values and belief in their role.

Bass located *transformational leadership* alongside the other two leadership styles which he described as:

- **Transactional**: Where leaders exert influence over their people by positive or negative reinforcement depending on their levels of performance.
- **Laissez-faire**: Where leaders abrogate responsibility for leading to subordinates.

Bass claimed that transformational leadership would transform followers to perform beyond expectations by creating an emotional bond between leader and follower and by arousing enthusiasm for a common vision. He suggested that transformational leaders could be characterised by their ability to motivate followers to follow.

TRANSFORMATIONAL LEADERS MOTIVATE FOLLOWERS THROUGH:

Idealised influence: Behaving in a manner that people will want to role model.

Inspirational motivation: Providing meaning, optimism and enthusiasm.

Intellectual stimulation: Encouraging followers to question old and ineffective routines and develop new, creative solutions.

Individualised consideration: Creating new opportunities for followers to be able to develop.

Bass argued that transformational leaders placed an emphasis on values and integrity and on recognising the needs, aspirations and potential contributions of their followers. This in turn, he claimed would get the most out of followers and lead to superior and sustained organisational performance.

HOW TO USE IT

Coaching someone to have the qualities described in Bass's model isn't going to be easy but, let's be honest, we're talking about some pretty heavy stuff here. I've encountered some leaders who just exuded charisma, some who were intimidating, some who attracted respect and others who were just plain frightening. All seemed to get the job done but each had a different impact on the people they were leading. Transformational leadership is not about manipulation or exploitation, but it is built on trust and integrity. Fail to convince the leader who you are coaching of this and you may as well go back to the drawing board. If the leader recognises your coaching will help them to develop as a leader, here are some tips to help you work with them:

- Get them to appreciate that, no matter how charming or charismatic they are, they must act in a manner based on sound ethical and moral values. Get them to accept that treating all of their followers with respect and integrity will result in their followers' trust and willingness to follow them without question.

- Show them that the best way to motivate their followers is by acting as a role model, setting high standards and getting their followers to believe in them (see Theory 22). If they do this they can expect staff to want to try and emulate them, at the very least never to let them down.

- Being able to stimulate followers requires the leader to have a degree of creativity. Not all leaders are creative. That's not a criticism, just a fact of life. Show them that they can be a great leader without being creative providing they take advantage of the creative talent that they have in their followers (see Theory 50).

- Get them to listen to and understand the needs of their followers (see Theory 17). Great leaders will act as coaches and mentors to their own staff so act as a role model yourself and show them how to be good coaches to their followers.

If you accept Bass's claim that transformational leadership would transform followers to perform beyond expectations by creating an emotional bond between leader and follower and by arousing enthusiasm for a common vision, then apply that principle to your role as the leader's coach.

QUESTIONS TO ASK YOURSELF

- How well have they accepted the need to change their leadership style?
- As their coach, am I always a good role model?

THEORY 58 RICHARD BOYATZIS: SELF-DIRECTED LEARNING

Use this when you want to recognise the freedom that clients have to learn.

Boyatzis argued that leaders often experience a tension between their individual growth and the expectations of their organisation. His theory of *self-directed learning* recognises the freedom that leaders have in deciding who they are and where they want to be. The theory is underpinned by five points of discontinuity where the leader experiences a moment of awareness that can provoke the need for change.

THE FIVE POINTS OF DISCONTINUITY CAN BE SUMMARISED AS:

Picturing the ideal self: This is the potential starting point in the process, where the leader discovers who they really want to be. This emerges from their image of the person they want to be, their dreams and aspirations.

Recognising the present self: This is the leader who others see and who they interact with. In this state, leaders often evoke self-defence mechanisms that protect them from the automatic intake of what others think about them.

Deciding what needs to change: The aim here is to create a learning agenda that not only caters for existing needs but can cope with future changes.

Experimenting with doing things differently: This is the point in the process where old habits are challenged and new habits start to emerge.

Developing productive relationships: Leaders need to develop relationships with people they trust to assist them in the process of change. To be effective, the relationships they form will need to give them a sense of identity and guide them towards what is appropriate and good behaviour.

Boyatzis argued that a leader's future is not entirely within their control, but most of what they become is within their power to create.

HOW TO USE IT

Boyatzis describes the process as an epiphany, a journey of self-discovery and turning points and makes the point that it is the individual's journey not the coach's. Here are some tips to help you with the process:

- At the first point of discontinuity ask the leader questions that encourage them to explore and formulate their ideal self. Get them to challenge the expectations and demands placed on them by their organisation. Don't underestimate the importance of the task that you have here. Skip over this stage and the whole process of self-directed learning collapses.

- Rationalising their self-image with what others see in them can prove to be difficult for some leaders who may have become deluded by their own sense of self-worth and ego. Your role at the second point of discontinuity is to bring them down to earth, but to do it slowly. At its most simple level, this involves you giving the leader feedback from your own observations and from the observations of others. Don't underestimate the practical difficulties involved in this in terms of the fear of exposure or criticism that the leader may feel or the sense of being put on the spot that others may feel.

- At the third point of discontinuity, recognise that leaders will only learn what they want to learn. They may even argue that they haven't reached a leadership position by not being able to discern between what's right and what's wrong for them and the organisation. Your role here is to help them bring a sense of realism to their learning agenda by getting them to examine their motivation for key aspects of the agenda and focusing on those aspects that will lead to the desired outcomes.

- The fourth point of discontinuity is what Boyatzis describes as the metamorphosis. Your role here is to create the conditions in which the leader can challenge existing habits and experiment on new ones in relative safety. Understanding what the leader's preferred learning style is (see Theories 2-4) and creating a sense of psychological safety (see Theory 17) will create an atmosphere in which leaders will experiment free from the risk of shame and embarrassment of failure.

- The fifth discontinuity is placed at the centre of the process. Most people will equate key moments of change in their lives to the support of an individual. Forging a relationship that supports the leader that is based on trust is therefore critical to the whole process.

QUESTION TO ASK YOURSELF

- Have I got the absolute trust and respect from the person I am coaching to enable them to describe the leader they want to be and the life and work they want in the future?

SECTION 2

BE BETTER THAN YOUR COMPETITORS

INTRODUCTION

The term *learning organisation* has become the label used for a conflux of ideas emerging from organisational research and practices since the early 1980s. It is, I suppose, a natural evolution of the quality management principles (see Theories 68–70) that were prevalent in the 1970s and more recent emphasis on values and beliefs (see Theories 62–64). Becoming a learning organisation is a critical step in what it takes to beat the competition.

Just what constitutes a learning organisation is, however, a matter of some conjecture, mainly because it is difficult to identify real-life examples of learning organisations. This is quite possibly because the vision is too ideal or because it doesn't match the requirements or culture of the organisation.

There does however seem to be agreement over the process by which the organisation becomes a *learning organisation*. Let's see if I can unravel what's meant here. Start with the notion that learning happens as a result of individuals wanting to change their behaviour through the acquisition of new skills, knowledge or insights. Organisational learning is the collective concern for learning by all members of the organisation acting on behalf of the organisation. The expectation here is that individuals act as *learning agents* for the organisation by identifying what needs to be done in order to transform the organisation into one which responds effectively to the needs of all stakeholders.

In this section, I have drawn on what I consider to be the seminal works on the subject of organisational learning. I have tried to balance what may appear to be quite complex theoretical models such as *triple-loop learning* and *systems thinking* with a basic overview of the different theories and some pragmatic steps for application.

If any of the entries appeal to you, and you have the time, then check out the recommended reading list at the end and get the books. I promise you won't be disappointed by any of them. I was so impressed by Pedlar, Burgoyne and Boydell's book (Theory 59) that I arranged to meet Tom Boydell. He didn't disappoint me and talked in a very modest manner about how the president of an African Country had approached him about turning his country into a *learning country*. I guess your undertaking is not going to be as grand as that but, believe me, it is just as important to the people who make up your organisation as it was to the people of that African country.

THEORY 59   # MIKE PEDLAR, JOHN BURGOYNE AND TOM BOYDELL: THE LEARNING COMPANY

Use this when you want to encourage the organisation to have a process for implementing and evaluating a transformation plan.

When Pedlar, Burgoyne and Boydell published their influential work *The Learning Company* (McGraw-Hill, 1997), they spawned a generation of public and private sector bodies wanting to be recognised as *learning organisations*. The principles underpinning the notion of the *learning company* were founded on the belief that such an organisation needed constantly to change to meet the needs of its customers and clients.

THE FIVE KEY AREAS TO ADDRESS ARE:

Strategy: This is where organisational policy and strategy formation, together with implementation and evaluation should be consciously structured as a learning process that involves all members of the organisation.

Intra-company learning: This involves promoting the notion that all departments see themselves as customers and suppliers to each other. In this respect they engage in constructive dialogue, negotiate and deliver excellent services to each other.

Organisational structures: The aim here is to create structures within the organisation that not only cater for existing needs but can cope with future changes.

Inter-company learning: This involves keeping a close look at what competitors and other organisations are doing and learning how their processes can be adapted and adopted to suit the organisation.

Learning climate: This is about encouraging people to share their knowledge and experiences with others and constantly look for professional and personal developmental opportunities of their own.

When the authors published the second edition of the book in 1997, they admitted that one of their basic principles was essentially flawed and that the idea that change needed to be done constantly was a potential recipe for chaos and disaster within an organisation. They suggested that the word *constantly* in their definition should be replaced with *consciously*: implying that, in order to be effective, the organisation needed to have an awareness of where it was and a willingness or desire to want the change. They also suggested that change needed to be incremental with periods of consolidation: a series of steps rather than a continuous curve.

HOW TO USE IT

This theory will help you to support the organisation to formulate a transformation plan together with a process for implementation, evaluation and improvement. It is not a gung-ho approach but one that allows them to develop, formulate and revise as they progress. Here are some steps to follow:

- Advise the organisation to start by forming a strategy group and getting them to define what the vision for the organisation is. A good method here is to describe this in terms of a metaphor. Use the same methods to describe where they are now and compare the two images and discuss how they can get from the present image to the vision. Get them to come out of the metaphor and into the real world by looking at the strengths and weaknesses within the organisation. Focus particularly on internal relationships, systems and structures. Ask, 'Do these help or hinder you achieving the vision?'

- Get them to look at what their competitors are doing. Establish benchmarks for products and services that they may be doing well that they should try to emulate or exceed. Then get them to look at what other organisations, not just their competitors who have similar processes as them (e.g. reception, finances, and human resource management), are doing and to establish benchmarks for processes that they may be doing that they should try to emulate or exceed.

- Get them to encourage a learning climate within their organisation by setting individuals up as role models and making resources and facilities for self-development available to all members of the organisation.

- Finally, suggest that the organisation finds a way of expressing their vision in a simple statement, or what's referred to as a *mission statement*. Something simple like, 'Good enough is not good enough, we always need to strive to do even better' will do.

If you don't like using metaphors in the exercises, then just skip that part of the process and focus on the real world.

QUESTIONS TO ASK YOURSELF

- Have I got the organisation to clearly define what the vision for the organisation is?

- Have I encouraged them to develop a learning climate within their organisation?

- What can I do to help them to benchmark what their competitors are doing?

THEORY 60

CHRIS ARGYRIS AND DONALD SCHÖN: TRIPLE-LOOP LEARNING

Use this when you want to help the organisation learn how to keep ahead of their competitors.

Argyris and Schön claim that organisational learning can be characterised in terms of a three-level evolutionary model consisting of single-, double- and triple-loop learning. That can be represented as:

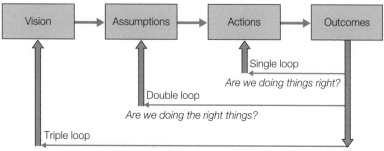

Source: Argyris, C. and Schön, D. (1974) *Theory in Practice: Increasing Professional Effectiveness*. San Francisco: Jossey-Bass.

THE CHARACTERISTICS OF SINGLE-, DOUBLE- AND TRIPLE-LOOP LEARNING ARE:

Single-loop learning is the basic level of quality control used by an organisation and is connected to error detection and correction. It asks the question: 'Are we doing things right?'

Double-loop learning is more geared to quality assurance and focuses on error prevention, throughout the organisation, not just at the point of delivery. It asks the question: 'Are we doing the right things?'

Triple-loop learning represents the highest form of organisational self-examination and involves constantly questioning services and determining where the organisation should position itself in the market place. It asks the question: 'How can we be sure what's right is right?'

Argyris and Schön argue that the triple-loop learning process incorporates a higher degree of creative input and that the organisational learning resulting from this is both an interactive and iterative process.

HOW TO USE IT

Although it's not just the quality of the product or service that dictates whether an organisation is outstanding, let's be honest this is at the heart of what they do and if they haven't got this right they may as well pack up. Too often the emphasis is built on the old quality control processes of *inspection–detection–rectification–retribution*: Let's look at what we're doing, let's detect errors, let's put them right and let's find out who's to blame. If this is what the organisation is doing they have stalled at single-loop learning. So, how do you help them out of the single-loop? Here are some things you, as their coach, can tell them:

- Do not get engrossed in the blame culture. Okay! So people make mistakes. The essence of double-loop learning is to learn from these mistakes. All right, if the same people keep making the same mistakes, you will have to do something about them.

- So, well done! By enthusiastic application of double-loop learning you have assured the quality of your products and services. Let's sit back and wait for the praise to roll in. Actually no! Your competitors have also read Argyris and Schön and have done the same. Someone in an underperforming college once asked me about another college which had been graded 'Outstanding' in their latest Ofsted inspection. 'What can we do to catch up with them?' they asked. I told them, 'I wasn't aware they were waiting for you'.

- Don't think that, like Bruce Banner transforming into the Hulk, transformation has to be that dramatic. It may be about addressing a few small things like changing the look of the reception area or how you deal with customers on the phone.

- Don't sit back and wait for things to happen. If this is the culture in your organisation, then do something about it and get out there and look for areas for improvement. It's important for you to learn from mistakes but it's also important to catch people out doing something good and see what you can learn from this.

The most important thing to tell the people you are coaching is that they don't have all the answers and to make sure that they involve others in the transformation process.

QUESTIONS TO ASK YOURSELF

- Have I impressed on them the importance of not sitting back and waiting for things to happen?
- Do they realise the importance of learning from mistakes?

THEORY 61 # PETER SENGE: THE FIFTH DISCIPLINE

Use this when you want to support the organisation to expand its capacity to create a better operational future.

Senge was influential in analysing what different organisations do to build learning capacity and why some organisations use learning better than others. He suggested five components, or disciplines, that must be followed to enhance the potential to create a successful environment for the organisation to learn.

THE CHARACTERISTICS OF THE DISCIPLINES ARE:

Personal mastery: This should be intrinsic and stem from a personal vision of effective operating.

Mental models: These are the beliefs, values and assumptions that form the basis of the personal vision.

Shared vision: This includes the shared and collective goals, values and mission that characterise the learning organisation.

Team learning: This is based on the belief that the intelligence of the team exceeds the intelligence of the individuals within the team.

Systems thinking: This discipline (the fifth one) is the conceptual framework for systems within the organisation that binds all of the other disciplines. It is the process of understanding how systems behave and interact with other systems.

Senge argued that it is important that all five disciplines are followed or else the depth of learning will be compromised.

HOW TO USE IT

If you want the people who you are coaching to be serious about creating a better operational future for their organisation, start by asking them: 'What do you want to create? What is your vision of an outstanding organisation?' Taking time early on to discuss this is crucial to build common beliefs, unleash people's aspirations and hopes and unearth reservations and resistances. Once you have established this here are some tips about how to progress:

- Make sure they are in tune with what's influencing beliefs, aspirations and resistances to change. Address all of these. Don't be afraid of challenging people about these beliefs. Doing this will help make people's mental models clearer for everyone and help to build shared understanding.

- Ask people 'How much do you actually know about yourself and the impact that your behaviour has on others?' Don't be afraid to encourage them to have this behaviour challenged. Use the communication techniques outlined in Theories 8–10 to demonstrate how they can enhance the quality of their interaction and relationships both inside and outside of their organisation.

- Encourage all members of the organisation to go through the same practices as above and reflect on how much they know about themselves and other members of the organisation. Make sure that they organise more robust and honest discussions within the organisation on the organisation's beliefs, values and mission.

- Okay, so this has started them thinking about their organisation. Tell them not to be fooled into thinking that the people who count are the usual suspects who turn up for monthly meetings. If that's how they think and have followed everything so far, tell them that they'll have great individuals or teams working in a rubbish organisation.

- Impress on them that no division in an organisation operates in a silo. Each division is interdependent on each other. An organisation will only be great if everyone involved wants to make it great.

QUESTIONS TO ASK YOURSELF

- Have I impressed on the organisation the need to define clearly what it is they want to create?

- Have I made a good enough job of challenging people about these beliefs and the assumptions they have about the organisation?

- Do they see the importance of learning as a collective body rather than an individual undertaking?

GET THE WORKPLACE CULTURE RIGHT

INTRODUCTION

The concept of culture in organisations has grown in significance over the past 20 years. This is partly because of dissatisfaction with the focus on the structural and technical aspects of the operating systems in some organisations and partly because of the shift in emphasis to the world of values and ideology.

But what exactly do we mean by *culture*? I once asked a group of middle-managers from a major car manufacturing company to tell me what culture meant to them. Their answers ranged from 'values and beliefs' to 'the blobby bits that grow in your cup over the weekend if you forget to wash it'. I acknowledged that values and beliefs certainly had an impact on culture, and that even the notion of penicillin growing in the cup suggested that culture was organic.

Writing this section was probably the most difficult section in the book. This wasn't because of a lack of good theories on the subject but because of a plethora of really great theories. In the *Little Book of Big Management Theories* (Pearson, 2013), we included eight entries on culture and could easily have doubled or trebled this. In this book I have restricted myself to just three entries. With such an embarrassment of riches how did I decide on the final entries?

I wanted entries that cover the spectrum of definitions that describe what the organisation *is* (the way it is perceived) and what the organisation *has* (its values and beliefs). I also wanted a theory that was taken from the traditional pragmatic approach and two from more contemporary *off-the-wall* approaches.

THEORY 62 | # EDGAR SCHEIN: THE THREE LEVELS OF ORGANISATIONAL CULTURE

Use this when you want to help an organisation to understand the values and beliefs it has.

Schein argues that the culture within an organisation is determined by a set of basic beliefs that the organisation has about itself that define what the organisation is. Schein believes that these beliefs are shaped by three separate entities which combine to form the culture of an organisation. These are:

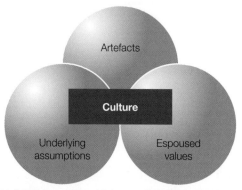

Source: Schein, E.H. (1992) *Organizational Culture and Leadership*. San Francisco: Jossey-Bass.

EACH OF THESE ENTITIES CAN BE DESCRIBED AS FOLLOWS:

Artefacts: These are the rituals, myths and legends that exist about the organisation which send out a message to the outside world about what makes the organisation a good or bad place to work in.

Espoused values: This is a set of guidelines (formal and informal) for managers and staff about what is acceptable behaviour.

Underlying assumptions: These are the often taken-for-granted understandings held by everyone about the organisation.

Schein's theory suggests that these entities can be consciously or subconsciously embedded in people's minds and, although they may be constructed, are no less real to those concerned.

HOW TO USE IT

Schein's work on culture is probably the most often quoted. He is sometimes referred to as the *founding father* of organisational culture.

Here are some tips to help you apply Schein's theory:

- To get the people you are coaching to understand the culture of their organisation, it's important firstly to understand how all stakeholders see the organisation. Encourage the organisation to start by taking a good look at the range of cultural clues that exist. A simple trawl around the organisation looking at how things work will be a good start.

- Get them to look first at the obvious: the surface manifestations. Get the organisation to ask key questions such as: 'If I was a worker here what would be my impressions about this organisation? Is this somewhere where I would like to work? Are work areas cluttered and untidy? Do people move and act in a business-like manner?'

- Get them then to dig deeper and check out values and basic assumptions. Stress that, in order to do this, they will need to talk to people. Choosing the method for doing this that is likely to get the best results is vital (see Theories 8–10). Face-to-face interviews are best but may be time-consuming. Workshops are great for dealing with large numbers but may not be confidential enough for some who may wish to express unpopular views.

- Once they have a good understanding of the organisation's culture, get them to make a judgement about how this fits in with their basic beliefs about what the organisation should be. A great way of doing this is to encourage managers to use a process called Management by Walking About (MBWA).

- Explain to the organisation that MBWA is a great way of keeping in touch with what people think about the organisation, but advise them that they shouldn't wander about aimlessly. Tell them to make sure that they have an objective for each walk and to listen and act on what people tell them. Here's a good example of this:

  A good friend of mine, and principal of a large college, gave up his office to the staff to use as a staff common room. He went on walkabout, sometimes sitting with staff in the common room, sometimes with learners in the refectory, sometimes with teachers in the classroom. He learned a lot about what staff and learners felt about the college. He also told me that he didn't get pestered with dozens of wasteful telephone calls and emails each day.

QUESTIONS TO ASK YOURSELF

- Is the organisation just settling on what's easy to see?
- How can I get them to dig deeper to find out about what people really think about the organisation?

THEORY 63 CARL STEINHOFF AND ROBERT OWENS: CULTURAL METAPHORS

Use this when you want to help the organisation to identify what people think their organisation is all about.

Steinhoff and Owens developed four metaphors (*Family, Machine, Circus* and *Little Shop of Horrors*), which they refer to as *phenotypes* that characterise the cultures that may exist in organisations. Here are the cultures, which I have categorised in terms of *Chaos* or *Control* and *Collective* or *Individual*:

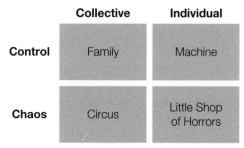

	Collective	Individual
Control	Family	Machine
Chaos	Circus	Little Shop of Horrors

I have adapted the metaphors to show how extremes can exist in each category.

THE METAPHORS FOR SHOWING EXTREMES ARE:

The Family: The organisation is viewed in terms of the relationships that exist there. They could be cosy and close-knit teams like the Waltons or dysfunctional like the Simpsons.

The Machine: The organisation is viewed purely in terms of a production line. This could be a well-oiled company, producing products of quality, such as Rolls-Royce (a car synonymous with the word 'quality') or the company that made the Trabant (described in one car magazine as a 'hollow lie of a car constructed of recycled worthlessness').

The Circus: The organisation is viewed in terms of the artistic and intellectual quality of its staff. Management are viewed as the masters-of-ceremony (keeping a watchful eye on performers) or show-stealers (placing their artistic ability above that of the other performers).

The Little Shop of Horrors: The organisation is viewed in terms of its unpredictability and chaotic nature. Organisations in this culture either have a Napoleonic complex (that promotes dominance and control) or Jekyll and Hyde personalities (that promote uncertainty and chaos).

HOW TO USE IT

Don't you just love using metaphors like this? No. Well you can't please everyone. If this isn't your cup of tea (sorry another metaphor) then skip this section. It's a shame if you do because getting people to use metaphors to make sense of their situations can be a very powerful and productive exercise.

- Start the process by using Steinoff and Owen's *phenotypes* to give people an insight into the use of metaphors. Getting them to compare their organisation in terms of the *Waltons* and *Simpsons* or *Rolls-Royce* and *Trabant* should be illuminating.

- Give each member of staff in the organisation (or small groups if you have a large organisation) some flip-chart paper and ask them to draw a picture of the organisation's culture. Don't be alarmed if you get your fair share of disturbing images (ants crawling over a dung heap and flowers with fangs are just some that I have seen).

- Ask the artists to explain what their pictures mean. Take each picture in turn and try to identify where the problems lie. Flowers with fangs are usually something to do with hidden menaces. I'll leave it to you to interpret other images. Try to get a feel from other members what they feel about the image and how to deal with it (pulling the fangs may address issues in the flower metaphor).

- At this stage don't be afraid to come back into the real world and start tackling some of the real issues. Maybe you can't get rid of the menace completely but you might be able to do something to reduce it.

Although I've used Steinhoff and Owens in this entry, there is a whole raft of great metaphors out there. Gareth Morgan, in particular, offers some great organisational metaphors in *Images of Organisations*. I suspect that I was taken by their use of the *Little Shop of Horrors* and the image that I had of my old college principal as a blood-sucking, flesh-eating plant. But that's another story…

QUESTIONS TO ASK YOURSELF

- Are the people who I am coaching comfortable using metaphors?
- What other methods could I use to get them thinking about the culture in their organisation?

THEORY 64   CHARLES HANDY: THE CULTURE GODS

Use this when you want to show an organisation how personalities can influence the culture of an organisation.

Handy suggests that the metaphor of Greek gods can be a useful way of depicting the personalities that influence how an organisation is perceived both internally and externally. These can be categorised in terms of: supportive/directive and concern for others/self-interest as follows:

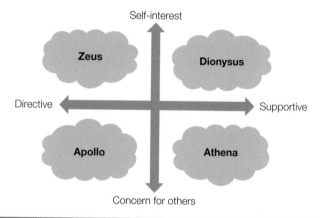

THE CHARACTERISTICS OF EACH OF THE GODS CAN BE SUMMARISED AS:

Zeus (web culture): Power is concentrated in the hands of one individual. Leaders are power driven, strong and charismatic.

Apollo (role culture): Power is hierarchical and defined in the roles people fulfil. Leaders are well-ordered and predictable, logical and analytical.

Athena (task culture): Power is derived from the expertise required to complete tasks. Leaders are wise, ambitious and good at solving problems.

Dionysus (existential culture): Power is with the individuals within the organisation. Leaders are self-interested and hard to influence.

Handy argues that, although an organisation may have a mixture of cultures, there will likely be one dominant culture.

HOW TO USE IT

Sorry if you hate football but I'm writing this entry as the end of the English football season is close with four teams fighting it out to become Premier League champions. Each of the four teams have managers with completely different personalities that, in turn, reflect the culture of their clubs.

- **Arsène Wenger**, manager of Arsenal FC, is the longest serving premiership manager, with an almost impregnable position at the club. In Handy's typology he would be a *Zeus*-like character operating a web culture where woe betide anyone who upsets him.

- **Manuel Pelligrini**, manager of Manchester City FC, is a relatively new manager at the club who has taken over one of the country's most expensive teams but has remained faithful to the structure established under the previous manager. He has a well-ordered and analytical approach to the game that Handy would probably classify as being like *Apollo*.

- **Brendan Rogers**, manager of Liverpool FC, is the new kid on the block whose problem was to pull together a club with great aspirations and some talented but wayward players. Rogers' ability to solve these problems and fashion together a team with championship potential would probably classify him as *Athena*.

- **José Mourinho**, manager of Chelsea FC, is nicknamed the *chosen one*. He has a squad of talented individuals who don't always function as a team. Handy would probably classify him as a *Dionysus* type because of his self-interest and hard-to-influence nature.

Use this model, and the soccer example, to make the organisation aware of the different cultures that exist within their organisation. Make the point that effective interventions must aim at striking a balance between the four cultures while remaining faithful to their dominant culture. Stress on them that effective organisations learn to build bridges between the various cultures that may exist within the organisation: creating cooperating rather than competing forces.

QUESTIONS TO ASK YOURSELF

- Does the organisation I am coaching have an insight into what cultures work best there?
- Are they aware of how leaders influence the organisation's culture?

SECTION 4

BE BETTER AT PLANNING

INTRODUCTION

I n the *Little Book of Big Management Theories* (Pearson, 2013), we offered 12 models of strategic management. The one thing all these models had in common was the importance of organisations getting to know the needs and expectations of their customers. Explain to the people who you are working with that, if they have responsibility for developing the organisation's business plan, then there are two types of planning that they will be involved in:

- **operational** planning that covers short-term decision-making;
- **strategic** planning that covers long-term development.

In this section I have looked at three models that are useful for either operational or strategic planning. Depending on the person's role in the organisation one of these models may be more relevant to them than the others, but all will be useful because having an understanding of the importance of short-term decision-making will impact on long-term strategic development and vice-versa.

THEORY 65 GERRY JOHNSON AND KEVAN SCHOLES: SEVEN STAGES OF STRATEGIC PLANNING

Use this when you want the organisation to identify key stages in the planning process.

Johnson and Scholes developed a seven-stage approach that they suggested would produce a comprehensive and structured strategic plan.

THE KEY POINT UNDERPINNING EACH STAGE ARE:

Mission: Have a vision of what the organisation should be like and a determination to get there.

Goals: Identify what goals must be achieved in order to realise the vision.

Objectives: Break down the goals into specific, measurable, acceptable, realistic and time-bound objectives.

Strategy: Determine what actions are necessary to achieve the objectives.

Actions: Execute the strategy.

Control: Set up a process for evaluating progress.

Rewards: Celebrate success.

Johnson and Scholes emphasised the role that key stakeholders have to play in each of these stages and in further research presented a stakeholder mapping model that categorised each stakeholder into their levels of power and interest.

HOW TO USE IT

Many of you will know of household names Chris Hoy and Bradley Wiggins. Both were knighted as a result of their services to the sport of cycling. Fewer will know about another cycling knight, David Brailsford: the genius (I never use that term lightly) behind the successes of British cyclists over the past five years. Brailsford has attributed these successes to the skills and knowledge he learned while studying for his MBA. I feel sure that at some stage in his studies he would have come across Johnson and Scholes because of his meticulous approach to planning.

This started with his audacious mission to win a pot full of world championship and Olympic gold medals and to do what no other British rider had come anywhere near to doing: win the Tour de France. His aim was to do this within five years; he achieved it in three. He set challenging objectives and relentlessly pursued the tiniest gains in everything: the bikes, the riders' fitness levels, their clothing, nutrition and teamwork. He referred to this as the aggregation of marginal gains. His attention to measuring these gains was evident when Wiggins crossed the line to become the first ever British winner of the Tour de France; he made sure that he punched the button on his data clock before punching the air with joy.

Can the organisation you are coaching match Brailsford? Can they clarify what is their vision for the organisation? Can they describe it clearly and graphically to everyone? If they have clarity of vision, here are a few tips to help them achieve this:

- Get them to specify the goals that they need to achieve to realise this vision. Do they want to increase the quality of products or services? Do they want to be more eco-friendly? Do they want to offer a wider range of products or services?
- Get them to break down the goals into specific, measurable, achievable, realistic and timely (SMART) objectives. Make sure that they have a process in place for measuring the progress of these objectives. Make sure that they identify who needs to be involved in achieving the objectives. Get them to specify tasks that individuals have to complete, monitor their performance and address any shortfalls in actual against planned performance.
- Impress on them the importance of not waiting until they have achieved the vision and encourage them to celebrate small successes *en-route* and recognise people's contributions. Easy achievement of the vision may mean the vision wasn't exciting or challenging enough and may lead to complacency. Failing to achieve the vision may mean that they were being over ambitious and may lead to despondency.

QUESTIONS TO ASK YOURSELF

- Have I convinced the organisation to have a clear vision of where they want to be?
- Have I helped them to define the goals they need to realise this vision in terms of the SMART acronym?

THEORY 66 **THE MCKINSEY GROUP: 7S FRAMEWORK MODEL**

Use this to demonstrate to an organisation how they can define and assess the viability of key elements in the organisation.

The 7S Framework was developed by a team working for the McKinsey Consulting Group. The model depicts the relationship between seven key elements that are essential in developing the well-being of any organisation. The interaction between the elements is usually demonstrated in the following diagrams:

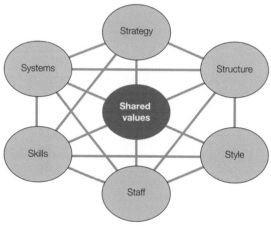

Source: Waterman, R.H., Peters, T.J. and Phillips, J.R. (1980) 'Structure is not organization', *Business Horizons* 23(3), pp. 14–26.

THE CHARACTERISTICS OF EACH ELEMENT CAN BE SUMMARISED AS:

Strategy: This is about having effective planning processes.

Structure: This is the way the various departments interact.

Style: This is how the organisation goes about its work.

Staff: This is how staff are recruited and developed in the organisation.

Skills: This is having the right skills mix in the organisation.

Systems: These are the procedures, processes and routines used within the organisation.

Shared values: This is the interconnecting heart of the model and is what the organisation stands for.

The McKinsey group suggest that changes in one element will create a chain reaction with others.

HOW TO USE IT

This isn't really as complex a model as it first appears. It just defines the key areas that are important within the organisation and stresses how each area impacts on the other six. The devil is in the application. To be used effectively you must encourage the organisation to take each element separately and ask a series of challenging questions:

- **Strategy**: Ask: (a) is planning in their organisation short-term, directionless and reactive? or (b) is there a clear vision of what needs to be achieved and how to achieve it?
- **Structure**: Ask: (a) is there confusion about who does what, poor inter-departmental communication and conflicting objectives? or (b) is there a clear understanding of where responsibility and accountability lie in the organisation, good inter-departmental communication and a common sense of purpose?
- **Style**: Ask: (a) are there sub-cultures that work independently and adopt different approaches? or (b) is there commitment to working cooperatively and a common approach?
- **Staff**: Ask: (a) is there a disparate approach to recruitment and lack of development opportunities? or (b) are there good processes for staff selection, motivation and development?
- **Skills**: Ask: (a) are people lacking the skills appropriate for the job? or (b) are skills appropriate for work to be done effectively?
- **Systems**: Ask: (a) do people pay lip service to these? or (b) does everyone adhere to them?
- **Shared Values**: Ask: (a) is there internal conflict and a lack of commitment to the vision? or (b) does everyone co-operate in working towards the vision?

If there is a tendency to favour the (a) responses in any element then you need to work with the organisation to think about how you can address this because it will drag everything else down. Favouring (b) responses however will start to have a positive effect on the other elements.

QUESTIONS TO ASK YOURSELF

- Have I convinced the organisation of the need to ask challenging questions in all aspects of the business?
- What must I do to make sure they act on responses to these questions?

THEORY 67 **MARY BITNER AND BERNARD BOOMS: THE 7PS MARKETING MIX**

Use this to demonstrate what an organisation needs to do to get its product or service to be successful.

The *marketing mix* is a famous planning tool used to describe the choices an organisation has to make when bringing a product or service to market. Bitner and Booms expanded on Jerome McCarthy's original 4Ps (Product, Place, Price and Promotion) to produce the following model:

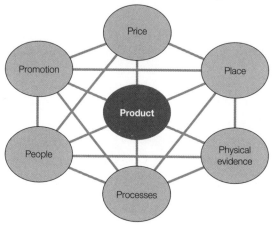

Source: Booms, B.H. and Bitner, M.J. (1981) 'Marketing strategies and organisation structures for service firms' in Donnelly, J. and George, W.R. (eds) *Marketing of Services*. Chicago, IL: American Marketing Association, pp. 47–51.

THE 7PS CAN BE SUMMARISED AS A SERIES OF KEY QUESTIONS:

Product: Is the organisation producing products or services that the market place wants?

Place: Can customers access the product or service when they need it?

Price: Has the organisation set a realistic value on the product or service?

Promotion: Is the organisation delivering the right message to the customers about the product or service?

People: Does the organisation have the right mix of skills to deliver a quality product or service?

Processes: Are the procedures, processes and routines used within the organisation efficient and effective?

Physical evidence: Do all customers and suppliers have the right image of the organisation?

Bitner and Booms emphasise the need to look at each of the Ps as inter-dependent of the other six. Having a great product that no one can afford or access or failing to have the right promotion or sales teams can be a recipe for disaster.

HOW TO USE IT

Standing in the middle of Tiananmen Square in Beijing you can see The People's Library, The Forbidden City, Mao's Mausoleum and a McDonald's sign. When McDonald's opened its restaurant in Moscow, the queues there were longer than those for Lenin's tomb. McDonald's marketing team don't always get it right though. When they launched their marketing campaign in China, they used their iconic clown Ronald as the centre of their campaign. Unfortunately they missed the point that the Chinese have difficulty pronouncing their 'Rs' and that the white face of the clown is symbolic in China as the death mask!

To help the organisation avoid making the same mistakes that McDonald's did in China, here are four basic steps to take:

- Convince the organisation of the need to research the market to make sure their product or service matches the needs of their customers.
- Get them to appreciate that it's one thing knowing what customers want, it's another thing having the right people and processes in place to deliver.
- Get them to look at each of the 7Ps variables in turn and determine what mix of activity will strike a balance between demand and supply.
- Finally, encourage them to keep on asking questions about the mix and making changes when necessary, until they are satisfied that it is the optimum mix.

In terms of marketing, McDonald's rarely gets it wrong but when it does, it does it *Big Mac* style.

QUESTIONS TO ASK YOURSELF

- Have I impressed on the organisation the importance of researching the market to ensure its product or service matches the needs of its customers?
- Has it looked at the variables and determined what mix of activity relative to the 7Ps will strike the right balance between demand and supply?

SECTION 5

MANAGE QUALITY

INTRODUCTION

Ask a group of people to give you the name of a quality watch or car and the likelihood is that products such as Rolex and Rolls Royce will feature high on the list. This is because there is a tendency to measure quality in terms of price and prestige. The implications of this are that most people, unable to afford such luxuries, will be deprived of quality. It is important therefore that we measure quality not in the above terms but relative to *fitness for purpose*: will the product or service do what we want it to and is it accessible in terms of price and availability?

Choosing the theorists for this section was arguably the easiest task in the book. Just as any discourse on philosophy leads back to the three great Greeks (Aristotle, Plato and Socrates), so I have no doubt that the three great Americans (Deming, Crosby and Juran) contributed more to our understanding of quality management in the 70s and 80s than anything else that followed. They did more than just write about the subject; they completely revolutionised the way industry and commerce thought about quality.

Deming's work in particular, in turning Japanese industry from a laughing stock into a byword for quality, was so impressive that I was compelled in the 1990s to sign up as a member of the Deming Society. He still remains the only Westerner to be awarded the Japanese Order of Merit for his work with industry. There is so much more in the work of Deming, Crosby and Juran than I have been unable to cover in this section, and that deserves further reading. If it is this aspect that you are coaching the organisation in, then there's enough here to get you started and some important points to cover with the organisation.

THEORY 68 **JOSEPH JURAN: THE 80–20 RULE – THE VITAL FEW AND THE TRIVIAL MANY**

Use this when you want to show the organisation how to avoid losing valued customers.

The 80–20 rule is sometimes referred to as *Pareto's Rule*. Pareto was an Italian economist who applied his rule to demonstrate that 80 per cent of the wealth in Italy was owned by 20 per cent of the population. It was Juran, one of the quality management gurus in the 1980s, who applied this rule to business to show the significance of *the vital few and the trivial many* and to demonstrate where an organisation needs to concentrate its efforts to maximise its results.

Juran argues that applying this rule to practice is simple.

FOR EXAMPLE:

80 per cent of an organisation's sales are probably being generated by 20 per cent of the organisation's customers, so concentrate efforts on the 20 per cent who are buying most of your products or services.

80 per cent of an organisation's staffing problems are likely to be caused by 20 per cent of its workers, so sort out the 20 per cent who are causing most of the problems.

80 per cent of an organisation's productivity may be down to 20 per cent of the workforce, so make sure you reward them accordingly.

Juran warns of settling for 80 per cent and moving on. He suggests that if the goal is just enough to get the job done, then 80 per cent effort may be enough. Success however can depend on what you do with the extra 20 per cent.

HOW TO USE IT

It's uncanny how often *Pareto's Rule* does crop up. That is of course if the organisation is willing to recognise that it's not a precise measure and accept that it could be 75/25 or 85/15. Stress on them that the one precious commodity they have is *time*, so work out how they can best deal with the *20-percentagers*. If these are the positive factors in the organisation then get them to explore ways that they can capitalise on this. If they are the negative factors, then get them to find out how to eliminate them, but make sure that when they deal with them, they do it in a professional manner.

I lere are some simple steps that you can get the organisation to take to make use of the 80–20 rule:

- Firstly, get them to identify the problems that they need to resolve.
- Then tell them to talk to staff, customers and suppliers to get their thoughts on these problems.
- Get them to score each problem on a scale of 1 (minor) to 10 (major).
- For each problem help them to identify what's causing this. Once the organisation has a good grip on the problems, get them to group problems together by root cause and to add up the scores for each group.
- Convince them to spend 80 per cent of their available time on taking action on the top 20 per cent of the highest scoring groups.

Stress on them that they can spend the remaining available time on the other 80 per cent of their problems but to keep in mind that low-scoring groups may not be worth the effort as solving these problems may cost more than the solutions are worth.

When I was asked by the principal of a college to help her introduce new measures into the organisation, I advised her of a slight variation on the 80–20 rule. This was that she would find 10 per cent of the staff would be avid supporters of her measures and 10 per cent would be avid opponents. Those staff in the two 10 per cent tails were basically fixed: the supporters were already on board and no amount of effort would convince the opponents to comply. I advised her to focus on the 80 per cent in the middle as they were the ones we needed to help push the measures through. She did this and the college went from a Grade 3 ('Adequate') Ofsted grade to a Grade 1 ('Outstanding') in the space of three years.

One word of warning: don't think that this principle implies that you only need to do 80 per cent of the work required!

QUESTIONS TO ASK YOURSELF

- How rigorously have I got the organisation to analyse its customer base?
- Have I succeeded in getting the organisation to focus on the 20 per cent of its customers who matter?

THEORY 69
WILLIAM EDWARDS-DEMING: 14 POINTS FOR QUALITY MANAGEMENT

Use this as way of showing the organisation what they must do to improve the quality of their products or services.

Deming was one of the most influential advocates of total quality management. He suggested that managers were 85 per cent responsible for the quality of their products or services and workers were 15 per cent responsible. He claimed that his *14 points* for how to manage quality would create a new way of thinking in organisations that would lead to greater customer satisfaction.

THE 14 POINTS CAN BE SUMMARISED AS:

Have a mission statement that all managers sign up to.

Don't accept excuses for mistakes, delays, defects and errors.

Don't depend on mass inspection to improve quality.

Only use suppliers who produce quality goods and services.

Look for continuous improvements in processes.

Provide appropriate training for all members of the workforce.

Institute participatory leadership.

Develop a climate of trust throughout the organisation.

Break down the barriers between departments.

Get rid of slogans and workforce targets.

Don't use arbitrary quotas that interfere with quality.

Remove barriers that prevent people from having pride in their work.

Encourage continuing professional development for everyone.

Get everyone's commitment to implementing the above points.

Deming argued that major improvements in the quality of products or services come from managers improving the system rather than workers improving their own performance.

HOW TO USE IT

I guess the question is, 'What's best – an organisation with great processes but a rubbish product or an organisation with rubbish processes but a great product?'

Here are some tips to use if this is an issue with the organisation that you are coaching:

- Get them to design products and services with quality in mind so that they meet customer demands and to design processes with quality in mind so that they work efficiently and effectively.

- Make sure that they recognise that quality depends on everyone so create teams of close knit and empowered workers. Get them to look for continuous improvement in processes and products. These may only be small ones but the accumulation of improvements can have a significant impact.

- Get them to appreciate that the organisation is part of both an internal and external supply chain with the quality of the final product depending on every link in the chain.

- Above all else, make sure that there is senior management commitment to the above steps.

For those organisations that say, 'We've always done it this way' and, 'If it ain't broke don't fix it', tell them, 'That's not good enough, you aren't looking close enough: fix it anyway'.

QUESTIONS TO ASK YOURSELF

- Have I impressed on the organisation that improvements in quality come from managers improving the system?
- Have I got senior management commitment to wanting quality improvement?

THEORY 70 PHIL CROSBY: THE MATURITY GRID

Use this as the basis for supporting an organisation to establish a quality programme.

Crosby was one of a number of *quality gurus,* including William Edwards-Deming and Joseph Juran, who sparked a quality revolution in the 1970s when they became the architects of the movement for Total Quality Management (TQM). He introduced two concepts which became key phrases in the TQM movement. The first was that *quality is free,* or more likely *unquality costs* in terms of warranty claims and bad public relations to organisations providing poor services. The second was the importance of *doing it right, the first time* and *every time.*

Underpinning these concepts was the importance of organisations reaching a level of operational maturity by progressing from *ignorance* and *uncertainty* to *wisdom* and *certainty.*

Uncertainty ➤ Awakening ➤ Enlighten-ment ➤ Wisdom ➤ Certainty

CROSBY'S MATURITY GRID CAN BE SUMMARISED AS:

Uncertainty: The organisation not knowing why it has issues with quality.

Awakening: The organisation starting the process of understanding why performance on these issues is low.

Enlightenment: The organisation devoting sufficient resources to resolving these problems.

Wisdom: The organisation preventing problems occurring in the first place.

Certainty: The organisation being confident that they are performing well on issues of quality.

HOW TO USE IT

As a fully paid up member of the Deming Society (yes, there is one), I feel a sense of treason using other models such as Crosby's model. I chose Crosby's model because I loved his analogy of quality having a lot in common with sex!:

Most people want more of it; everyone believes they understand it; everyone thinks they are good at it; and we all believe that any problems are caused by other people.

To help an organisation to apply this theory:

- Get them to start by building alliances with all managers and support staff in the organisation who have a commitment to offering a quality provision.
- Encourage them to have a feel for where the organisation is on the journey from *uncertainty* to *certainty* (there's a format for testing this in Crosby's *Quality is Free* (Penguin, 1980)).
- Tell them not to panic if the response indicates their organisation is in the lower levels of the grid (*awakening*).
- Get them to accept that there are problems and that only by accepting the reality of these will they be able to do something about them (*enlightenment*).
- Encourage them to develop a system that prevents issues with quality occurring rather than just responding to them (*wisdom*).

Now that I've shown you how to sort out their quality problems, let's talk about sex!

QUESTIONS TO ASK YOURSELF

- How aware am I of where the organisation stands on the maturity grid?
- Have I impressed on the organisation that moving from uncertainty to certainty about the quality of products or services involves awakening, enlightenment and wisdom?

SECTION 6

RESPOND TO CHANGE

INTRODUCTION

Many people find change painful and/or inconvenient: preferring to stay in their comfort zones or failing to understand the reasoning behind it. Each of us differs in the way we perceive change: what may be fresh and stimulating to one person may be a major disruption to another. We also differ in our abilities to face the unknown and deal with the uncertainty that change brings. I don't think that for one minute this section will deal with all of the issues that you face as someone going through or managing a change process. What it will do is to give you a greater understanding of the issues that people face while going through change and some useful tools to help you manage a change programme.

Leading change however isn't easy. It involves reviewing and understanding both the internal and external environment for the trends that can impact on the organisation. Some of the trends can have a positive effect on the organisation but others can frustrate the process. In *The Little Book of Big Management Theories* (Pearson, 2013), we looked at eight unique models of change management. We also included sections on more traditional tools for environmental scanning such as SWOT and PEST analysis which will prove invaluable to those involved in leading change. If there are common elements running through all of these models, then these can be summarised as:

- It is important to establish that change is necessary: make sure that the evidence and data back up the need for change.
- Each person perceives change differently: be aware that some consider it fresh and stimulating, whereas others are terrified by the thought of change.
- Planning for change from a solid base is essential: be clear about *how* to change as well as *what* to change.
- Effective communication is critical: it is vital to share the vision and outcomes expected as a result of change.

For the purpose of this section, I have used three models that cover change from an organisational as well as a personal perspective.

THEORY 71 **JOHN KOTTER: EIGHT-STEP APPROACH**

Use this to get the organisation to appreciate that building the proper foundations for an effective change programme is essential.

Kotter suggested that leadership of change entails establishing direction, aligning people and then motivating and inspiring them to implement the planned change. He proposed an eight-step model.

THIS CAN BE SUMMARISED AS:

Establish a sense of urgency: Identify the challenges facing the organisation.

Form essential coalitions: Get the right people on board who have the power to implement change.

Develop a vision for change: Link your plans for change with an exciting vision that people will identify with.

Communicate the vision: Talk about the vision frequently and enthusiastically with staff and customers.

Remove obstacles: Modify or, if necessary, get rid of any people, processes or protocols that undermine the vision.

Generate short-term wins: A few early success stories will inspire everyone to keep going.

Build on the wins: Don't get complacent if performance improves, keep focused on the long-term.

Embed changes: Make the changes part of the organisational culture

Kotter suggested that hard work, careful planning and building strong foundations were essential ingredients for a successful change programme.

HOW TO USE IT

As a business coach, advise the organisation that planning change is always easier than implementing it. If they ask 'why?' tell them it's because articulating what they want to do involves scanning data and analysis, whereas implementing it involves people. Even Kotter's model emphasises the need to encourage people to have some input and encourages them to have a sense of ownership of the process. Here are some tips on how to use this model effectively:

- Get the organisation to start by having a clear understanding of what needs to be done and how people will be affected by the change. Tell them not to just look at numbers but at what perception people have of the need for change.
- Encourage them to appoint a *change agent* who will champion the change process and to identify who the key people are who can support the change process and get them to work with the *change agent*.
- Make sure they have a clear vision of what they want their organisation to be. See if you can get them to express this in one statement. Some people refer to this as a vision statement but ruin it by having a half-page statement of intent. The devil's not in the detail (that can follow) but in the clarity of vision.
- Help them to look at what obstacles (people, processes or protocols) may exist to restrict change and get them to either modify them or, in extreme circumstances, get rid of them.
- Support them to get a few inexpensive, quick wins under their belt. Warn them that some failures or unintended consequences can be a good learning experience so encourage the organisation to get these into the open as well. Tell them that these quick wins are not the beginning of the end, merely the end of the beginning so get them to consolidate on these and keep firmly focused on the long-term. Warn them that this may take time.

  A friend of mine is managing director of an old established metal-fabricating company. He told me that he knew he was changing the outlook of his workers when the first thing that they did in the morning was to 'switch on their machines before they switched on the kettle'. It had only taken him five years to get to that point!

QUESTIONS TO ASK YOURSELF

- Have I impressed on the organisation the importance of having a clear understanding of what needs to be done and how people will be affected by the change?
- Have they expressed this in terms of a vision of the future organisation?
- Have they appointed a suitable *change agent* who will champion the change process?

THEORY 72 ELISABETH KUBLER-ROSS: THE GRIEF MODEL

Use this when you want to help the organisation to understand people's reactions to change.

Kubler-Ross described five reactions that reflect the way people react to tragic news. She suggested that the reactions were *coping mechanisms* that were normal for people to go through before acceptance of the news could be achieved.

EACH OF THESE REACTIONS CAN BE SUMMARISED AS:

Denial: A conscious or unconscious sense of disbelief and a refusal to accept change. Physical responses to this may include numbness and shock.

Anger: As people start to accept change as a reality, denial turns to resentment or fear. They may need to vent their anger at others or to internalise it and go through a process of self-recrimination.

Bargaining: This is the turning point as someone's acceptance of change grows. They will start to test and explore what the change means to them and either resolve problems or put off the inevitable.

Depression: If bargaining hasn't worked, the reality of the situation sets in. At this point, people will become more aware of any losses associated with the change. They may feel down and depressed.

Acceptance: This is where people realise that fighting change is not going to make it go away. People reaching this point have a resigned attitude towards the change and a willingness to get on with it.

Kubler-Ross explained that people don't go through the stages one at a time in a neat step-by-step manner. Some people will stall in one particular stage and can even move back into stages that they have been in before.

HOW TO USE IT

In the steps that follow explore your role in coaching the organisation in this process:

- **Denial**: No matter how well the change has been planned and how much you know it is important to the organisation, you must convince the organisation to appreciate that people need time to adjust. Get the organisation to discuss the change proposals with staff as soon as possible. Get them to make sure they give them the necessary information, and support them in helping them to understand the implications of what's happening and where they can get further help.

- **Anger**: This the *danger zone* for all concerned. Tell the organisation that if they mess up here they may free-fall into crisis or chaos. Make sure that they have carefully considered the impact and concerns that their people have. Warn them that they may not be able to pre-empt all of the objections but making sure they listen carefully to what people have to say and observing their reactions will help minimise their anger.

- **Bargaining**: This may be the turning point for the organisation and individuals. Warn them however that it is not the beginning of the end, merely the end of the beginning. Successful outcomes in this stage will propel people to *acceptance*. Tell them not to be complacent though because, if they fail to resolve problems during the bargaining process, people may regress back to *anger* or drift into *depression*.

- **Depression**: Advise them to look for the signs of demotivation and uncertainty. People may quit or become unproductive. Sickness and absenteeism rates may increase. It may not be the end of the proposed change but it will take the organisation a lot of soul-searching to decide if they are going to abandon the change or see if people reluctantly accept it.

- **Acceptance**: If people have reached this stage from *bargaining* then tell the organisation they can be confident that they have their people on board. If people are there from *depression* they may have a resigned attitude to the change and a reluctant acceptance that it is going to happen. This may not be a happy time for all concerned, so advise the organisation to deal with it sensitively. Make sure they appreciate that they may be a victim of the next change.

Now think about two issues where you had to handle change. Choose one that had a positive result and one that had a negative result.

QUESTIONS TO ASK YOURSELF

- What did I do that had an impact on whether the result was good or bad?
- Could I now have handled it differently?

THEORY 73 **JOHN FISHER: THE TRANSITION CURVE**

Use this when you want to help the individuals in an organisation to use reflection as a prelude to change.

Fisher argues that how an organisation deals with change depends on who initiated the change and what control they have over the events in question. He suggests that no matter how small the change, it has the potential to have a major impact on individuals within the organisation, their self-view and subsequent performance. He describes this impact in terms of a series of transitional events that can be depicted as:

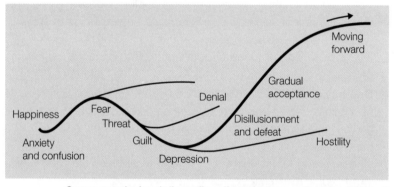

Source: **www.businessballs.com/freepdfmaterials/processoftransitionJF2012.pdf**

EACH OF THESE REACTIONS CAN BE SUMMARISED AS:

Anxiety and confusion: The awareness that events lie outside of your control.

Happiness: The awareness that your feelings are shared by others.

Fear: The awareness that change is imminent. This could lead to your lack of acceptance of any change and *denial*.

Threat: The awareness that change will impact on your core behaviour.

Guilt: The awareness that your past behaviour was questionable. This could lead to awareness that your beliefs and values are incompatible with those of the organisation and a sense of *disillusionment* and *defeat*.

Depression: The awareness that a lack of motivation and confusion is setting in. This could lead to a failure to see where things are going and *hostility*.

Gradual acceptance: The awareness that you need to do something positive in order to start *moving forward*.

Fisher warns of the conflicts that people may face when challenging existing values and beliefs and the dangers of getting too engrossed in the emotion of the change which may result in missing vital signs of threat, fear and anxiety.

HOW TO USE IT

To help an organisation to move through the transition effectively, you need to understand their perception of the past, present and future. You need to ask, 'What are your past experiences of change? How did you cope with this? What will you be losing or gaining as a result of the change?' You may not be able to change this perception so concentrate your efforts on supporting them to work through the implications for themselves. Encourage them to do some soul-searching and to reflect on why they are feeling the way they are.

Smith Brothers Engineering had built up a good reputation for quality bespoke engineered components for the aerospace industry, with 80 per cent of their work with one customer. Unfortunately, due to a fall-off in orders, they were faced with the threat of closure.

The problem was that management and workers were unable to adequately picture the future. Everyone knew that change was essential but had avoided openly discussing how to go about this. This had resulted in rumours and anxiety and confusion.

They resolved the issue by making everyone redundant. Those that wanted to would invest their redundancy payments in forming a workers' cooperative. The company would then rent out their premises and equipment to the cooperative which would work on existing aerospace contracts, but would also have the freedom to negotiate contracts with other companies.

This was a massive culture shock to all concerned in the business but, as the cooperative is still trading, one that worked.

QUESTIONS TO ASK YOURSELF

- How well have I encouraged people to reflect on their past, present and potential future experiences?
- Am I dealing effectively with people's feelings of fear or hostility to change?

SECTION 7

WORK TOGETHER

INTRODUCTION

We are not by nature good team members. Watch a pack of wolves in one of David Attenborough's wonderful wildlife series isolate a weaker member of a herd of buffalos and move in for the kill and you may think that we could learn much about how other animals work as a team. See the same pack fight viciously over a small morsel of food and you may think otherwise.

In order for people to find a reason to work as a member of a team, they need a common purpose and a sense of identity. Put a group of people in a lift together and they think and act as individuals. Create a crisis situation (a breakdown or fire) and the need for survival becomes the common purpose, with each individual assuming a role (comforter, problem solver etc.). Moving from mere survival as a team to effective operation and optimum performance is a process that requires understanding, commitment and great leadership.

In this section I want to look at the three components of that process. I look firstly at Belbin's theory about the roles that you need for a team to be effective and then at Tuckman's theory about the process that a team needs to go through to become effective. The section is completed by a look at the impact that certain personality types can have in their role as team manager. Understanding how these three theories work and how they could be used in tandem to create a great team is what a good coach needs to support the organisation to be working towards.

THEORY 74 **MEREDITH BELBIN: TEAM ROLES**

Use this when you want to help the organisation to understand the roles that people play within a team.

The principles that underpin Belbin's work are simple: in order for teams to be successful, certain functions or roles must be undertaken. Belbin suggests that certain roles must be filled for effective teamworking to exist.

BELBIN'S ROLES ARE:

Co-ordinator: Sets the agenda for team meetings, clarifies team objectives, establishes priorities and facilities discussion.

Shaper: Drives the team towards its objectives, engenders a sense of urgency and maintains momentum.

Plant: Comes up with original ideas.

Monitor Evaluator: Analyses what the team are committing themselves to and measures progress objectively.

Implementer: Turns strategy into action.

Resource Investigator: Finds the resources necessary to achieve objectives and susses out what the opposition are up to.

Team Worker: Helps to settle issues (personal as well as professional) within the team and helps the team to gel.

Completer Finisher: Has a key role to play towards the end of the project when people are flagging and work needs polishing.

Specialist: Provides technical expertise in key areas.

Belbin acknowledges that people may be expected to fill more than one role, especially in smaller teams and that duplication of certain roles can lead to conflict within the team.

HOW TO USE IT

The Great Escape (1963) is a film based on a true story about a special stalag, or prison camp, built by the Germans in 1944 to house troublesome prisoners-of-war. With the common purpose of escape, the prisoners begin to work as a team: Squadron Leader Bartlet (played by Richard Attenborough) co-ordinates activities: Captain Hilts (played by Steve McQueen) proves to be the driving force behind people's desire to escape: Lt Velinski (played by Charles Bronson) is the expert on tunnelling: Lt 'Scrounger' Hendley (played by James Garner) gets the materials they need to make things work: Lt Blythe (played by Donald Pleasance) is responsible for making the forged passports.

Stress on the organisation that it's important that they need to constantly analyse what's going on and identify both problems and their causes. For example:

- If there's a lack of awareness of where the team is at a given moment and what needs to be done to move it forward then ask them if they have the right *Co-ordinator*.
- If there's a lack of clarity about the team's objectives and how it will achieve them, and if the co-ordinator is not to blame, then get them to check out their *Shaper*.
- If there's an inability to come up with new ideas, ask them what the team *Plant* is doing.

Tell them that if they have identified a problem within the team, they have to deal with it. Tackling poor performance is not easy and, in the final analysis, warn them that they may have to expel an existing member from the team. By the way, please don't remind them that most of the escapees in the film were caught and shot!

QUESTIONS TO ASK YOURSELF

- Does the team have the right mix of people to be effective?
- What must I do too as the team coach to make sure all of the team roles are covered?

THEORY 75 BRUCE TUCKMAN: THE TEAM DEVELOPMENT MODEL

Use this when you want to help the organisation to understand at what stage in their development the team is.

Tuckman suggested that teams go through a five-stage developmental process before they become a fully operational performing team. The stages are:

EACH OF THESE STAGES CAN BE SUMMARISED AS:

Forming: This is where members start to interact with each other and work out what is expected of them. Some members of the team will feel excited and enthusiastic in this stage, while others will feel afraid and uncertain.

Storming: As people start to mingle, conflict occurs as personal agendas start to emerge. Some members will assert themselves and begin to question authority, while others will go along with what's being said.

Norming: As the members of the group find ways of resolving conflict they begin to emerge as a cohesive unit. Criticisms are constructive and the team members start to work cooperatively with one another.

Performing: As confidence and trust in each other begin to grow, performance levels increase.

Adjourning: As the task has been completed, the group dissolves. At this stage, team members will either feel a sense of satisfaction or loss, depending on the outcome. Other emotions may include relief or sadness.

Tuckman stressed the importance of providing guidance to the team at the very outset of the team formation. He argued that clarity of objectives and roles would be a major factor in determining whether early emotions would be based on excitement or fear.

HOW TO USE IT

Tuckman's first and middle names were Bruce and Wayne. In team-building parlance, he is undoubtedly a *superhero*! Here are some tips as to how the organisation should react in each stage of the team formation process:

- As the group begins to *form*, advise the organisation that the team manager needs to meet with the group members both individually and collectively to discuss ground rules. Suggest that the manager explains what it is that they expect from the team and answer any questions team members have.

- In the *storming* stage, warn the organisation that they can expect conflicts over values and challenges to their manager's authority. If disagreements get too heated then advise the manager to remain calm and deal with incidents assertively as they occur as acting aggressively or passively will not achieve much.

- If the manager has dealt effectively with the *storming* phase, the team will enter the *norming* stage and begin to develop their own ways of dealing with disagreements. Advise the manager that this is the time to start backing-off.

- If all has gone to plan, the team will start *performing* as a cohesive unit. Suggest that the organisation keeps a watchful eye on proceedings but stress the importance of allowing the manager and the team space. Advise the organisation not to be concerned if the team makes mistakes but to support them to learn from the mistakes.

- Once the task has been completed, celebrate the team's achievements and acknowledge everyone's contribution. Advise the organisation to do this even if the team's ultimate goal wasn't achieved.

QUESTIONS TO ASK YOURSELF

- How aware am I of what stage in their development the team is at?
- What can I do to coach them through the next stage?

THEORY 76 **ICHAK ADIZES: TEAM MANAGEMENT PERSONALITY STYLES**

Use this when you want the organisation to have the right mix of team management skills.

Adizes suggested that team management roles can be categorised into one of four personality styles (*Producer, Administrator, Entrepreneur* or *Integrator*). These can be represented in terms of perspective (internal or external) and results (short-term or long-term) and depicted as follows:

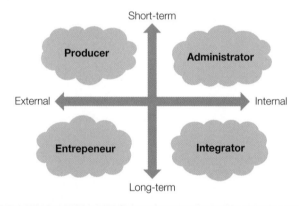

EACH OF THESE STYLES CAN BE SUMMARISED AS:

Producer: High-energy active people who are focused on getting tangible results. They dislike finer details, ambiguity or abstract thinking.

Administrator: Quiet, cautious people who need to know the details of processes or procedures before committing themselves. They dislike ambiguity or uncertainty.

Entrepreneur: Imaginative and charismatic people who focus on novel challenges and exciting opportunities. Usually typecast as dreamers, they can get easily bored.

Integrator: Great at organising and resolving internal conflicts. In attending to team members' personal needs, they can sometimes get distracted from the task.

Adizes argues that, although most people develop skills in all four areas, nobody can be equally strong in all four areas. He maintains that everyone has at least one dominant style, and sometimes a secondary style which may also be nearly as strong as the dominant style.

HOW TO USE IT

As we reach the last entry in the book, the really exciting news is that they have decided to make a film of this book. George Clooney (well, it is my book) is being considered to play the Author's role and Uma Thurman the Editor. We have to choose a Director. The contenders (with their Adizes' classifications) are:

- **Woody Allen** (*Producer*): Actors complained of Allen's cold and aloof demeanour.
- **Alfred Hitchcock** (*Administrator*): Hitchcock demonstrated that he was the master of exacting detail. He sketched every shot of the movie himself, leaving nothing to chance.
- **Walt Disney** (*Entrepreneur*): Walt Disney was both creative and a perfectionist. His famous saying about, 'If you can dream it, you can do it', typified many of his films.
- **Quentin Tarantino** (*Integrator*): Tarantino chose his leading actors on the basis of if he enjoyed their company over lunch, they were in.

Use the model, and the film director's analogy, to describe how different personality types can have an impact on how the organisation performs. Here are two key points to stress if you are using this model:

- Don't be alarmed if the manager who you are coaching is not naturally gifted in all four styles. It doesn't indicate any frailties on their part. Indeed, there may even be mileage in supporting them to concentrate on developing their strongest style(s) rather than on becoming an all-rounder.
- If you are coaching a team manager who clearly lacks some of the style qualities required by an organisation and who may lack the ability to adapt to the required style, then get them to face up to this and try to get the organisation to team the manager up with someone who will complement their style. If this is possible then, for this action to be effective, each of the partners must respect the different values and priorities of the other person and appreciate that different styles will use different tactics to achieve a desired outcome.

Please let me have your thoughts on who we should choose for the Director (yes I know some of them aren't still alive). My Screenwriter's Academy Award acceptance speech is ready.

QUESTION TO ASK YOURSELF

- Does the manager I am coaching have the right style required by the organisation?

SUMMARY OF PART 3

In Part 3, I have tried to look at a number of theories that have an impact on the way that the organisation responds to operational needs. It's the capacity to respond in this way that a number of theorists argue is the feature that defines a *learning organisation*. The three models of the *learning organisation* depict how organisations develop the organisational structure and people in a way that promotes clarity, involvement and competitiveness.

The entries relating to coaching organisations on managing culture, strategy, quality, change and teams have been presented in a way that will enable you to analyse what needs to be done and how to go about doing it.

The key points to emerge from this part of the book are to convince the organisation:

- That their ability to learn faster than their competitors may be the only sustainable competitive advantage that they have.
- It's important for them to have a clear vision of where they want the organisation to be and to involve everyone in the process of getting there.
- To make sure that they express the vision for the organisation in a simple statement of intent.
- If they need to make changes to the way the organisation goes about doing things, they must dig deep to find out about the underpinning values and assumptions that people have about the organisation.
- Getting people to express their feelings about the organisation in terms of a metaphor can be a very enlightening exercise.
- Achieving a vision of what the organisation could be is more of a journey than a destination.
- Making changes in one aspect of the organisation will have a positive or negative impact on other aspects.
- Any plans for change should consider and respect individuals' ideas of what the organisation should look like.
- Not to let people perceive that change is something that's being done to them.
- That 80 per cent of their problems may be down to 20 per cent of their people.

- That 80 per cent of their sales may be from 20 per cent of their customers.
- That moving from uncertainty to certainty about the quality of products or services that an organisation offers includes awakening, enlightenment and wisdom.
- Everyone in the organisation has a role to play in quality improvement.
- That teams go through key development phases and they need to know at which stage their teams are.
- Different management styles will use different tactics to achieve different outcomes.

A FINAL WORD ON COACHING

I hope that you have found something that you can use in this book, either as a manager or a coach. Here are some general tips to emerge from the various sections to help you along the way:

- **Clarify the role**: Establish who does what, when, where and how. Discuss what expectations you and the people being coached have of each other. Agree the ground rules and boundaries for the coaching relationship.

- **Organise goals and objectives**: Get the people you are working with to have a vision about what they could be and set goals that will help them to achieve this vision. Make sure these goals are SMART (specific, measurable, acceptable, realistic and time bound). Have sessional objectives as well as long-term goals.

- **Act with conviction**: Choose the most appropriate method for coaching an individual/group. This may involve directing them, showing them what to do, suggesting ways they can do it or stimulating them to do it themselves. Whatever method you choose, see it through with conviction and commitment.

- **Confirm that expectations are being met**: Don't think that this is something you do at the end of the coaching session: it should be done frequently throughout a session. Elicit feedback not just on the outcome but on the process undertaken and be prepared to make changes if necessary.

- **Have a strategy for dealing with setbacks**: Accept that bad things happen. This might be lacking the resources to support a client, having to deal with conflict or finding that there is opposition to your ideas or methods. It's how you deal with these incidents that will define you as a person as well as a coach. Reflecting on why bad things happen and what you could do next time to avoid them is important, but having the ability to think on your feet and deal with them when they do occur is just as important.

- **Inspire creative thinking**: Encourage the person you are coaching to be willing to think outside of the box. Great ideas or learning experiences rarely happen as a result of people doing the same thing over and over again. Coaching people to be competent is okay, but supporting them to be creative is where the real value lies.

■ **Never be afraid of failure**: If the person you are coaching fails at a task, it doesn't mean that you or the individual is a failure: it simply means that they have failed the task. Get them to analyse why they failed the task and what they can do differently next time. Make sure that if they fail the task again they do it better than the time before. If the failure is down to your coaching then it's up to you to analyse what you can do differently.

■ **Get to know the person you are coaching**: Build a relationship that is based on respect and trust. If you have this relationship, you can challenge someone, set difficult tasks or ask provocative questions, both secure in the knowledge that this is being done with good intent.

I hope that you have enjoyed reading this book as much as I've enjoyed writing it. Please share with me any thoughts that you have by emailing me: **saddlers9899@aol.com**.

What did you think of this book?

We're really keen to hear from you about this book, so that we can make our publishing even better.

Please log on to the following website and leave us your feedback.

It will only take a few minutes and your thoughts are invaluable to us.

www.pearsoned.co.uk/bookfeedback

RECOMMENDED READING

Theory 1: Knowles, M. (1988) *The Modern Practice of Adult Education: From Pedagogy to Andragogy.* Cambridge, UK: Cambridge Book Company.

Theory 2: Fleming, N.D. (2001) *Teaching and Learning Styles.* Honolulu: VARK-Learn.

Theory 3: Kolb, D. (1984) *Experiential Learning: Experience as the Source of Learning and Development.* Englewood Cliffs, NJ: Prentice-Hall.

Theory 4: Myers, I.B. and Briggs, K. (1975) *The Myers-Briggs Type Indicator.* Palo Alto, CA: Consulting Psychologist Press.

Theory 5: Keller, J.M. (2010) *Motivational Design for Learning and Performance: The ARCS Model Approach.* New York: Springer.

Theory 6: McGregor, D. (1985) *The Human Side of Enterprise.* New York: McGraw-Hill.

Theory 7: Herzberg, F. (1966) *Work and the Nature of Man.* Cleveland: World Publishing.

Theory 8: Argyle, M. (2004) *Bodily Communication*, 2nd edn. East Sussex: Routledge.

Theory 9: Berne, E. (1964) *Games People Play: The Psychology of Human Relationships.* London: Penguin.

Theory 10: Luft, J. and Ingham, H. (1955) *The Johari Window: A Graphic Model of Interpersonal Awareness.* Proceedings of the Western Training Laboratory in Group Development. Los Angeles: UCLA Extension Office.

Theory 11: Bloom, B.S., Engelhart, M.D., Furst, E.J. *et al.* (1956) *Taxonomy of Educational Objectives: The Classification of Educational Goals. Handbook I: Cognitive Domain.* New York: David McKay Company.

Theory 12: Dave, R.H. (1970) 'Psychomotor levels' in Armstrong, R.J. (ed.) *Developing and Writing Behavioral Objectives*. Tuscon, AZ: Educational Innovators Press.

Theory 13: Krathwol, D., Bloom, B.S. and Masia, B.B. (1973) *Taxonomy of Educational Objectives: The Classification of Educational Goals. Handbook II: Affective Domain.* New York: David McKay Company.

Theory 14: Pavlov, I. (2003) *Conditioned Reflexes.* Mineola, NY: Dover Publications.

Theory 15: Guthrie, E.R. (1959) 'Association by contiguity' in Koch, S. (ed.) *Psychology: A Study of a Science,* Vol. 2. New York: McGraw-Hill. pp. 158–95.

Theory 16: Merton, R.K. (1968) *Social Theory and Social Structure.* New York: Free Press.

Theory 17: Maslow, A.H. (1943) 'A theory of human motivation', *Psychological Review* 50(4), pp. 370–96.

Theory 18: Rogers, C. (2004) *On Becoming a Person.* London: Constable.

Theory 19: Mezirow, J. (1997) 'Transformative Learning: Theory to Practice', *New Directions for Adult and Continuing Education* 74, 5–12.

Theory 20: Barber, P. (2001) *Researching Personally and Transpersonally: A Gestalt Approach to Facilitating Holistic Inquiry and Change in Groups and Organisations.* Guildford: Work Based Learning, School of Educational Studies, University of Surrey.

Theory 21: Pribram, K., Miller, G.A. and Gallanter, E. (1960) *Plans and Structure of Behaviour.* New York: Holt, Rinehart & Winston.

Theory 22: Bandura, A. (1977) *Social Learning Theory.* New York: General Learning Press.

Theory 23: Hebb, D.O. (1949) *The Organization of Behavior: A Neuro-psychological Theory.* New York: Wiley and Sons.

Theory 24: Festinger, L. (1957) *A Theory of Cognitive Dissonance.* New York: Harper & Row.

Theory 25: Merzenich, M. (2013) *Soft-wired: How the New Science of Brain Plasticity can Change your Life*, 2nd edn. San Francisco, CA: Parnassus Publishers.

Theory 26: Lewin, K. (1951) *Field Theory in Social Science: Selected Theoretical Papers* (Edited by D. Cartwright). New York: Harper & Row.

Theory 27: Honey, P. (1994) *101 Ways to Develop Your People Without Even Trying.* Maidenhead: Peter Honey Publications.

Theory 28: Hare, R.D. (2003) *The Psychopathic Checklist – Revised*, 2nd edn. Toronto: Multi-Health Systems.

Theory 29: Bandler, R. and Grinder, J. (1979) *Frogs into Princes.* Moab, UT: Real People Press.

Theory 30: Bateson, G. (1973) *Steps to an Ecology of Mind.* Boulder, CO: Paladin Press.

Theory 31: Broadbent, D. (1958) *Perception and Communication.* Oxford: Pergamon.

Theory 32: Brounstein, M. (2000) *Coaching and Mentoring for Dummies.* Hoboken, NJ: Wiley Publishing.

Theory 33: Costa, A. and Kallick, B. (1983) 'Through the Lens of a Critical Friend', *Educational Leadership* 51(2): 49–51.

Theory 34: De Bono, E. (1978) *Teaching Thinking.* Harmondsworth: Penguin. De Bono, E. (1985) *Six Thinking Hats.* New York: Little, Brown and Company.

Theory 35: Dilts, R. (1994) *Strategies of Genius Volume 1.* Capitola, CA: Meta Publications.

Theory 36: Egan, G. (2014) *The Skilled Helper: A Problem Management and Opportunity-Development Approach to Helping*, 10th edn. Belmont, CA: Brooks-Cole.

Theory 37: Fournies, F.F. (2000) *Coaching for Improved Work Performance.* New York: McGraw Hill.

Theory 38: Gallwey, T. (1986) *The Inner Game of Tennis.* London: Pan McMillan.

Theory 39: Gardner, H. (1993) *Multiple Intelligence: The Theory in Practice.* New York: Basic Books.

Theory 40: Gilbert, A. and Whittleworth, K. (2010) *The OSCAR Coaching Model.* Monmouth, Wales: Worth Consulting Ltd.

Theory 41: Goleman, D. (1998) *Working with Emotional Intelligence.* London: Bloomsbury.

Theory 42: Grimley, B. (2013) *Theory and Practice of NLP Coaching.* London: Sage.

Theory 43: Grinder, J., Bandler, R. and Delozier, J. (1977) *Patterns of the Hypnotic Techniques of Milton Erickson Volume II.* Capitola CA: Meta Publications.

Theory 44: Hale, R. and Hutchinson, E. (2012) *Understanding Coaching and Mentoring.* London: MX Publishing.

Theory 45: Hawkins, P, (2006) *Coaching, Mentoring and Organizational Consultancy.* Maidenhead: McGraw-Hill.

Theory 46: Kabat-Zinn, J. (2004) *Wherever You Go, There You Are: Mindfulness Meditation for Everyday Life.* London: Piatkus Books.

Theory 47: Landsberg, M. (2003) *The Tao of Coaching.* London: Profile Books.

Theory 48: Lane, D. and Corrie, S. (2006) *The Modern Scientist-Practitioner: A Guide to Practice in Psychology.* East Sussex: Routledge

Theory 49: McCleod, A. (2006) *Performance Coaching.* Bancyfelin, Wales: Crown House *Publishing*.

Theory 50: McPhedran, A. (2009) 'Turning Ideas Into Reality', **www.trainingjournal.com** (accessed 15 August 2014).

Theory 51: Parsloe, E. and Wray, M. (2008) *Coaching and Mentoring: Practical Methods to Improve Learning.* London: Kogan Page.

Theory 52: Rogers, J. (2004) *Coaching Skills: A Handbook*. Maidenhead: McGraw-Hill.

Theory 53: Satir, V. (1988) *The New Peoplemaking.* Palo Alto, CA: Science and Behavior Books.

Theory 54: Sweller, J. (1994) 'Cognitive Load Theory: Learning difficulty, and instructional design', *Learning and Instruction* 4(4): pp. 295–312.

Theory 55: Whitmore, J. (1998) *Coaching for Performance*. London: Nicholas Brealey.

Theory 56: Adair, J. (1979) *Action Centred Leadership*. Farnham, UK: Gower.

Theory 57: Bass, B.M. (1985) *Leadership and Performance Beyond Expectations.* New York: Free Press.

Theory 58: Boyatzis, R.E. (2013) 'Coaching With Compassion: Inspiring health, well-being, and development in organizations', *The Journal of Applied Behavioral Science* 49(2): pp. 153–78.

Theory 59: Pedlar, M., Burgoyne, J. and Boydell, T. (1997) *The Learning Company.* Berkshire: McGraw-Hill.

Theory 60: Argyris, C. and Schön, D. (1974) *Theory in Practice: Increasing Professional Effectiveness*. San Francisco: Jossey-Bass.

Theory 61: Senge, P. (1992) *The 5th Discipline*. London: Century Business.

Theory 62: Schein, E.H. (1992) *Organizational Culture and Leadership*. San Francisco: Jossey-Bass.

Theory 63: Steinhoff, C. and Owens, R. (1989) 'The Organizational Culture Assessment Inventory: A metaphorical analysis in educational settings', *The Journal of Educational Administration* 27(3): pp. 17–23.

Theory 64: Handy, C. (1996) *The Gods of Management.* New York: Oxford University Press.

Theory 65: Johnson, G. and Scholes, K. (2005) *Exploring Corporate Strategy,* 7th edn. Harlow, Essex: Financial Times Prentice Hall.

Theory 66: Waterman, R.H., Peters, T.J. and Phillips, J.R. (1980) 'Structure is not an organization', *Business Horizons* 23(3), pp. 14–26.

Theory 67: Booms, B.H. and Bitner, M.J. (1981) 'Marketing strategies and organisation structures for service firms' in Donnelly, J. and George, W.R. (eds) *Marketing of Services.* Chicago, IL: American Marketing Association, pp. 47–51.

Theory 68: Juran, J. (1951) *Quality Control Handbook.* New York: McGraw-Hill.

Theory 69: Deming, W.E. (2000) *Out of Crisis.* Cambridge Mass: MIT.

Theory 70: Crosby, P. (1980) *Quality is Free.* London: Penguin.

Theory 71: Kotter, J.P. (1990) *A Force for Change: How Leadership Differs from Management.* New York: Free Press.

Theory 72: Kubler-Ross, E. (1969) *On Death and Dying.* Toronto: Macmillan.

Theory 73: Fisher, J.M. (2003) *The Process of Transition and the Transition Curve*: see **www.businessballs.com** [accessed 1 December 2014].

Theory 74: Belbin, R.M. (1993) *Team Roles at Work.* Oxford: Butterworth Heinemann.

Theory 75: Tuckman, B.W. (1965) 'Development sequences in small groups', *Psychology Bulletin* 3(6): pp. 384–99.

Theory 76: Adezis, I. (1991) *Corporate Lifecycles*. Stockholm: Liber Publishing.

INDEX